NOIR CITY

OFFICIAL MAGAZINE OF THE FILM NOIR FOUNDATION

No. 41 | 2024

PUBLISHED BY THE FILM NOIR FOUNDATION

San Francisco | Los Angeles | New York

NOIR CITY

ISSUE 41

PUBLISHER Eddie Muller

EDITOR IN CHIEF Imogen Sara Smith
MANAGING EDITORS Danilo Castro,
Steve Kronenberg
ART DIRECTOR/DESIGNER Michael Kronenberg
PROMOTIONAL DIRECTOR Daryl Sparks
CONTRIBUTORS THIS ISSUE Dan Akira, Carsten Andresen,
Sean Axmaker, Mary Mallory, Jason A. Ney, Kenny Reid,
M.T. Schwartzman, Drew A. Smith, Matthew Sorrento,
Stefen Styrsky, Rachel Walther
COMMUNICATIONS DIRECTOR Anne Hockens
WEBSITE / E-SERVICES Ted Whipple

FILM NOIR FOUNDATION BOARD OF DIRECTORS
Eddie Muller, President; Board members:
Foster Hirsch, Brian Hollins, Andrea Kasin,
Anita Monga, Alan K. Rode

ADVISORY COUNCIL Dana Delany, Gwen Deglise,
James Ellroy, Bruce Goldstein, Vince Keenan, John Kirk,
Dennis Lehane, Leonard Maltin, Rose McGowan, Jon
Mysel, Fernando Martín Peña, Michael Schlesinger,
Imogen Sara Smith, Todd Wiener

FILM NOIR FOUNDATION

The Film Noir Foundation is a non-profit public benefit corporation created by Eddie Muller in 2005 as an educational resource regarding the cultural, historical, and artistic significance of film noir as an international cinematic movement. It is the foundation's mission to find and preserve films in danger of being lost or irreparably damaged, and to ensure that high-quality prints of these classic films remain in circulation for theatrical exhibition to future generations. Once these films are unearthed, restored, and returned to circulation, the chances increase that the films will be made available on Blu-ray and/or via online streaming for future generations of film lovers to appreciate.

To date, the Film Noir Foundation has fully funded the restorations of *The Prowler* (1951), *Cry Danger* (1951), *Try and Get Me!* (1951), *Too Late for Tears* (1949), *Woman on the Run* (1950), *The Guilty* (1947), *Los tallos amargos* (1956, Argentina), *The Man Who Cheated Himself* (1950), *Trapped* (1949), *La bestia debe morir* (1952, Argentina), and *El vampiro negro* (1953, Argentina), and *The Argyle Secrets* (1948). The Foundation has initiated and partially underwritten the restoration of *Repeat Performance* (1947) and *High Tide* (1947), and financed 35mm preservations of *Nobody Lives Forever* (1946), *Three Strangers* (1946), *High Wall* (1947), *The Hunted* (1948), *The Window* (1949), *Southside 1-1000* (1950), *Roadblock* (1951), *Down Three Dark Streets* (1954), *Loophole* (1954), *The Underworld Story* (1950), and *Cry Tough* (1959), plus the Argentine films *Apenas un delincuente* (1949), *No abras nunca esa puerta* (1952), and *Si muero antes de despertar* (1952). The Film Noir Foundation's latest restoration, *No abras nunca esa puerta* (1952, Argentina), premiered opening night of NOIR CITY 21, January 19, 2024, at Oakland's Grand Lake Theatre, and will screen at 2024 NOIR CITY satellite festivals.

NOIR CITY, the FNF's Bay Area flagship festival, began in January 2003. It has grown into the largest film noir–specific yearly event in the United States, the centerpiece of the Film Noir Foundation's public awareness campaign. Viewers have been drawn to this NOIR CITY every year (except 2021) from all over the world, eager to immerse themselves in a extravaganza of rare films, special guests, music, literary tie-ins—a communal celebration of all things noir.

Please consider supporting our mission with a donation to the Film Noir Foundation.

NOIR CITY.
THIS ISSUE
NO. 41 | SUMMER 2024

*Clicking title
jumps to article

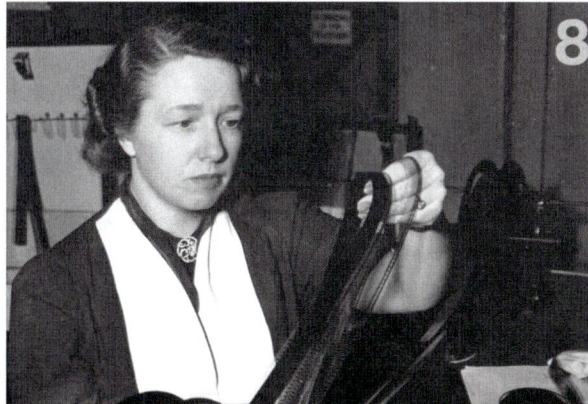

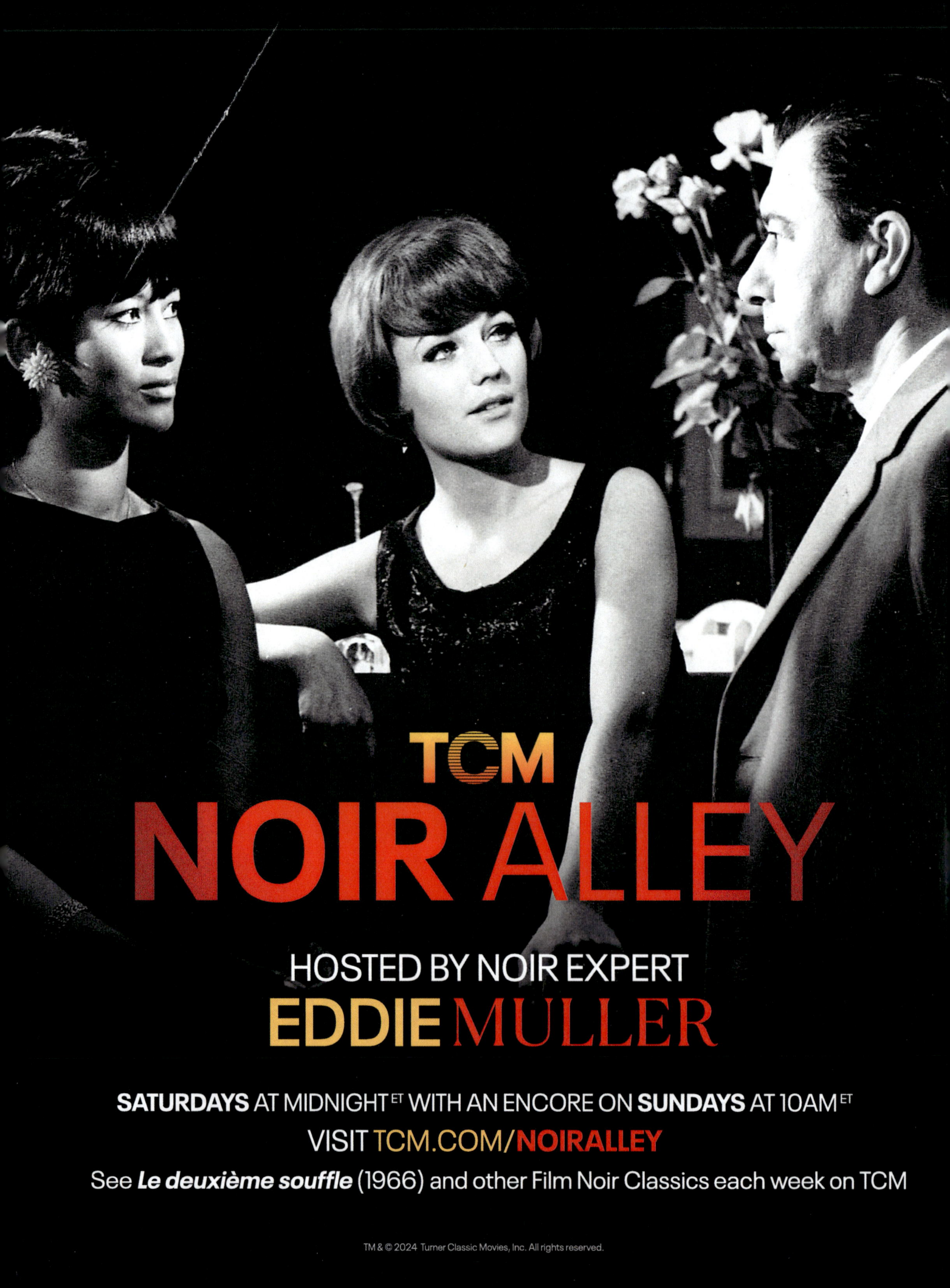

TCM
NOIR ALLEY

HOSTED BY NOIR EXPERT
EDDIE MULLER

SATURDAYS AT MIDNIGHT^ET WITH AN ENCORE ON **SUNDAYS** AT 10AM^ET

VISIT TCM.COM/**NOIRALLEY**

See *Le deuxième souffle* (1966) and other Film Noir Classics each week on TCM

LETTER FROM THE EDITOR

Summer tends to be a season for movies that invite you to turn off your brain: IP-driven, CGI-laden franchises and Hollywood's usual array of remakes, reboots, and retreads. Here at *NOIR CITY*, we're pushing back with a summer issue that ventures into the unfamiliar and the overlooked, airs some dissenting opinions, and encourages readers to step out of their comfort zones. The issue features four first-time contributors and a tribute to a movie none of our creative team had ever heard of when it was pitched to us (Alberto Rodríguez's *La isla mínima* [aka *Marshland*, 2014]). Elsewhere, Jason Ney unearths a true crime backstory stranger than fiction, while Stefen Styrsky and Steve Kronenberg explore the murky regions where film noir overlaps with horror and science fiction to plumb the mysteries of identity. Matthew Sorrento reviews a book that provocatively pushes the boundaries of classic noir up through the 1960s.

In studio-era Hollywood, film editing was an art that hid in plain sight, as skillful cutters tried to ensure that audiences wouldn't notice their work. Adding to the profession's invisibility, many of its leading practitioners were women. Mary Mallory profiles Viola Lawrence, a pioneering cutter who became one of the pillars of Columbia Pictures, the scrappy studio that punched above its weight and celebrates its centennial this year. If Lawrence is remembered today, it is often as the scissors-wielding villain who butchered Orson Welles's *The Lady from Shanghai* (1948) on orders from mogul Harry Cohn, who allegedly offered a thousand bucks to anyone who could explain the convoluted story to him. The tale of the film's tortured production and postproduction is no less complex, but Mallory argues that Lawrence's work did more to salvage than defile what critic Dave Kehr has called "the weirdest great movie ever made."

Over the years, *NOIR CITY* has explored the presence of coded queer characters in classic noir films. Back in 2010 (when this publication was still the *Noir City Sentinel*) our longtime contributor and award-winning crime novelist Jake Hinkson wrote about the lesbian presence in film noir, and in 2021 our frequent book reviewer Randy Dotinga explored how Hollywood smuggled gay themes past censors to create "Lavender Noir," which earned Randy a SoCal Journalism Award. In this issue, two pieces look at what has happened since those wink-wink characters came out of the closet. Drew Smith, a graduate student in NYU's Martin Scorsese Department of Cinema Studies, argues that Rose Glass's *Love Lies Bleeding* (2024) marks a breakthrough for the femme fatale and opens new roads for queer neo-noir. Carsten Andresen reevaluates William Friedkin's *Cruising* (1980), a film that on its release provoked furious protests from the gay/BDSM community it depicted and remains intensely controversial. An associate professor of criminal justice at St. Edward's University, Carsten draws on his study of crimes against the LGBTQ community in his defense of the film as a groundbreaking, and rule-breaking, police procedural.

Disagree with something you read here? Couldn't agree more? Let us know. Beginning with our next issue, we will publish a selection of readers' letters, and we welcome your compliments, comments, and thoughtful criticism. You can write to editor@filmnoirfoundation.org, and include LETTER TO THE EDITOR in the subject line. No blackmail, poison pen, or ransom notes, please.

Film noir teaches us many useful lessons, such as always to leave the motor running during a heist, and never to trust a crooked cop. It also instructs us on how to live with ambiguity and mixed feelings. This is a skill that seems to have gone the way of fedoras and rotary telephones in our hyper-polarized culture, but we at *NOIR CITY* believe things are rarely black and white, even—or especially—in those black-and-white movies we call noir.

Darkly yours,

Imogen Sara Smith

—*Imogen Sara Smith*

"Once you get trapped, there's no escape from them. Girls like Susan never learn!"

CONTRIBUTE

Film noir's rain-slicked streets, shadowy alleys, and sex bombs in silk peignoirs deserve a permanent place on the BIG screen. But hey, "it's a bitter little world," and we can't do it alone. We need your donations to help us locate, restore, and exhibit these films before they're lost forever. Do it for the love of noir—but enjoy the thank-you gifts, too!

HOW TO CONTRIBUTE TO THE FILM NOIR FOUNDATION
Please see contribution levels listed on the right and the associated gifts for each.

NOTE: If no gifts are desired, you may indicate such and you will receive a 100% tax deduction.

Option 1 - Make your donation ONLINE from the FNF's contribute page via PayPal (yes, you can use your credit card) at https://www.filmnoirfoundation.org/contribute.html

Option 2 - Make your donation via CHECK and mail to:

Film Noir Foundation
1411 Paru Street
Alameda, CA 94501

Important: IN ORDER TO RECEIVE THE NOIR CITY E-MAG, DONORS MUST SIGN UP ON THE FNF MAILING LIST at **https://www.filmnoirfoundation.org/signup.html**

Note: Does your PayPal address differ from your mailing list email address? If your PayPal email address differs from the email address provided for our mailing list, be sure to let us know, so you will be included in the NOIR CITY e-mag broadcasts.

PLEASE ALLOW AT LEAST FOUR WEEKS FOR DELIVERY OF DONOR THANK YOU GIFTS. Be sure to provide your mailing address to receive merchandise. Apologies, but we cannot ship donor thank-you packages outside the United States

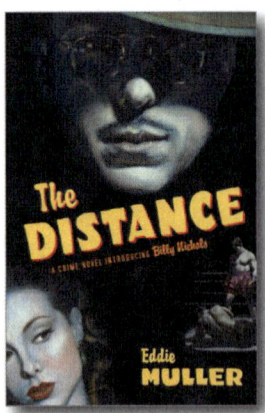

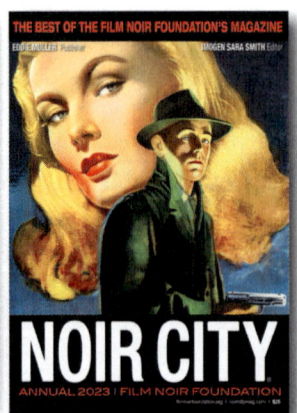

Get the NOIR CITY® e-magazine
A donation of $20 or more entitles you to receive a 1-year subscription to the *NOIR CITY* e-magazine, published every four months in electronic format, and sent as a downloadable link in an email to donors who have signed up on the mailing list. IMPORTANT: You must sign up for the *NOIR CITY* e-magazine at filmnoirfoundation.org/signup.html in order to receive the electronic publication.

SHAMUS
$20 to $49
Receive the *NOIR CITY* Magazine - digital version (e-mail address required).

MUSCLE
$50 - $99
Receive the *NOIR CITY* Magazine - digital version - and the most recent NOIR CITY festival poster.

HENCHMAN
$100 - $249
All of the above, plus the 2024 NOIR CITY 21 Souvenir Program and a copy of the NOIR CITY Annual 16 (releasing late September 2024).

TORPEDO
$250 - $499
Receive all of the above plus a signed first edition of Eddie Muller's novel, *The Distance*.

KINGPIN
$500+
The whole shebang plus a NOIR CITY Passport (all-access pass) to NOIR CITY 22 at Oakland's Grand Lake Theatre in January 2025. January 2025 10-day festival dates TBD.

THE
CRITERION
CHANNEL

A Noir Lover's Dream

Niagara, directed by Henry Hathaway

Queen of the Cutters

Did VIOLA LAWRENCE Mangle a Masterpiece . . . Or Did She Salvage *The Lady from Shanghai*?

By Mary Mallory

She may have looked like a sweet, kindly matron, but editor Viola Lawrence had a spine of steel, which she proved working with some of the most temperamental if talented directors in film history: Erich von Stroheim, John Ford, Howard Hawks, Nicholas Ray, and Orson Welles. She even managed volatile Columbia Pictures chief Harry Cohn with aplomb. Lawrence also made a significant mark in film noir, cutting multiple crime pictures as well as the movement's first 3-D movie, *Man in the Dark* (1953). She made considerable contributions to two of noir's most venerable titles: *The Lady from Shanghai* (1947) and *In a Lonely Place* (1950). Although she's mostly forgotten today—except when the tortured production history of Welles's film is recounted—her sharp focus on pacing and close-ups contributed to shaping these masterpieces.

Born on December 2, 1894, in Brooklyn, inquisitive Viola Mallory came of age during the development of motion pictures as a burgeoning entertainment business. At eleven, she became a messenger for nearby Vitagraph Studios, eventually graduating to cutting and conforming negatives. As apprentice to Vitagraph's lead editor, Frank Lawrence, Mallory edited her first movie, a three-reeler, in 1912, making her perhaps the first female film editor in the United States.

Women were the first cutters in the industry, and they continued to dominate the field throughout the studio era. They were seen as well suited to the precise, detail-oriented work and sensitive to the ways that creative editing could flesh out stories. Although men eventually entered the profession, women such as

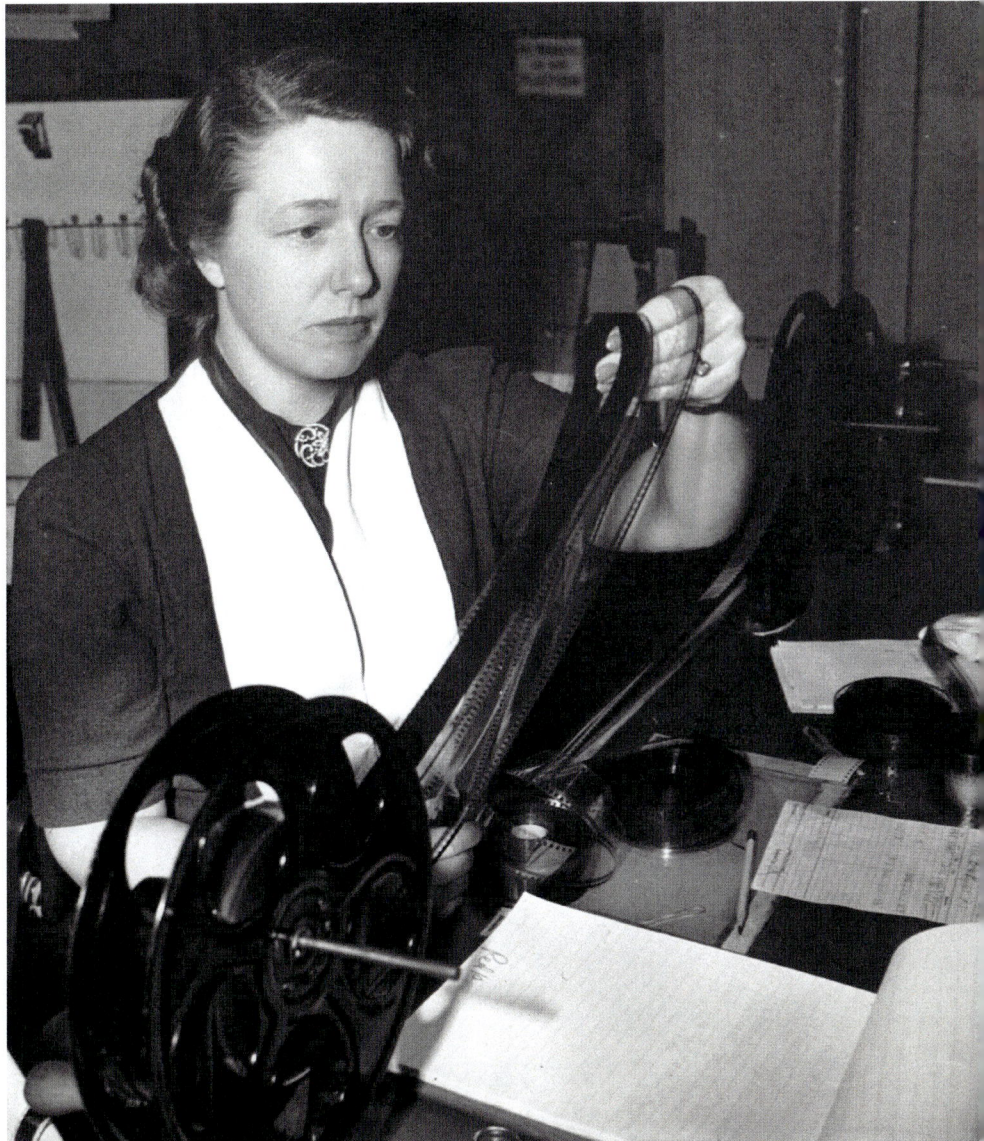

Viola Lawrence at her Columbia Studios editing table, circa 1935. Courtesy Pollak Library, Cal State Fullerton

Margaret Booth, Barbara McLean, Blanche Sewell, Anne V. Coates, and Dede Allen were esteemed editors in the industry for decades.

Mallory followed Frank Lawrence west in 1917, into Universal Studio's San Fernando Valley editing department, where she worked on von Stroheim's first film as director, *Blind Husbands* (1919). Newspapers reported that "the best titling and editing brains have been turned loose" on the film. Mallory's poise and strength impressed Frank Lawrence so much that in 1918 he married her. The following year he made his wife the head of the editing department.

During the next decade, Lawrence gained a reputation for her modern approach to cutting, using close-ups and adding visual clues to enhance the dynamism of movie storytelling. Cohn, impressed by her professionalism, made her the head of his fledgling studio's editing department in 1925, but her growing renown led to many projects beyond Columbia's confines. She edited films for Samuel Goldwyn

Viola Lawrence as a young woman on her way to editing success, circa 1920. Courtesy Pollak Library, Cal State Fullerton

and worked on some of diva Gloria Swanson's independent productions, including a salvage job on the unfinished *Queen Kelly* (1932), directed by the talented, if arrogant, von Stroheim. Unhappy with the director's indulgent approach, Swanson (who produced the film with Joseph P. Kennedy) cut von Stroheim loose. Interweaving the fired director's sophisticated footage with more prosaic and static sequences—some including sound—Lawrence (with fill-in director Richard Boleslawski and cameraman Gregg Toland) fashioned a new ending and managed to streamline the unwieldy film to 101 minutes, allowing circulation in Europe and South America for a project once deemed unfit for release. (It was not released domestically, where von Stroheim maintained contractual control, but a clip from the film appears in *Sunset Boulevard* [1950]).

At Cohn's request, Lawrence returned to Columbia in the 1930s to act as the

Part of the *Blind Husbands* editing staff for Erich von Stroheim's debut as director. Grant Whytock, left, von Stroheim, Viola Lawrence, and Frank Lawrence

A seething Queen Regina V (Seena Owen) chases and whips servant girl Kitty Kelly (star Gloria Swanson) after catching her in the palace prior to her wedding to Prince Wolfram in von Stroheim's *Queen Kelly*. Lawrence's editing partially salvaged the debacle and allowed a European release. Courtesy of Mary Mallory

studio's chief editor. She displayed an ability to remain affable, self-possessed, and assertive when handling stressful personalities and situations, qualities Cohn found invaluable. Top-line directors such as Frank Borzage, John Ford, and Dorothy Arzner sought out her services, noting that she was a pleasure to work with; actor Chester Morris even autographed a still of himself to Lawrence with the inscription, "Thanks for being so sweet." Others found her cool and ruthless, at least in the cutting room; actress Ann Sheridan declared that Arzner and Lawrence "leave their femininity outside when they pick up their cutting shears."

Lawrence's dedication to tight storytelling and fast-paced, invisible editing meshed perfectly with director Howard Hawks's masculine style of filmmaking, contributing to the success of his aviation adventure *Only Angels Have Wings* (1939). Though editors were rarely singled out for their contributions, she likely deserves credit for the qualities that the 1939 industry survey *The Movies . . . and the People Who Make Them* saw in Hawks's film, which it called "highly melodramatic . . . with convincing, staccato dialogue and terse, taut scenes that move with speed and precision to create excitement and suspense."

IN 1947, LAWRENCE FACED her greatest challenge when confronted with the task of assembling Welles's *The Lady from Shanghai*, a deliciously mad adult fairy tale that Cohn regretted ever greenlighting. The story of a naive sailor (Welles) drawn into a globe-trotting tangle of deceit by a beautiful but duplicitous siren turned glamorous Rita Hayworth (then Welles's wife) into one of noir's coldest seductresses. In the ensuing years, Welles and his many aco-

> "Others found her cool and ruthless, at least in the cutting room; actress Ann Sheridan declared that Arzner and Lawrence 'leave their femininity outside when they pick up their cutting shears.'

The Lady from Shanghai's dramatic fun house sequence, with puzzled Michael O'Hara (Orson Welles) confronting the duplicitous Elsa Bannister (Rita Hayworth).

lytes would decry Lawrence's supposed desecration of his film; a case can also be made that she brought desperately needed cohesion to a production that had spiraled out of control.

The seasoned editor had lived through this before, with von Stroheim. Both directors were visionaries, full of flair and romanticism, whose films featured fatalistic humor and a sardonic view of life. But both men also exhibited petulant, egotistical, and extravagant behavior that could sabotage their projects. Legend has it that Cohn was incensed by Welles's initial rough cut, exclaiming in the screening room, "I'll give a thousand dollars to anyone who can explain this f$#@ing thing to me!" That person would essentially be Lawrence, who had the skill and disposition to do her job while mediating headstrong bulls like Welles and Cohn. Welles later lambasted her work, but Lawrence's editing brought a brisk pace and a semblance of narrative cohesion to the atmospheric film, while retaining—and perhaps at times *enhancing*—the director's signature brashness and ingenuity.

The Lady from Shanghai is a convoluted fun house of gorgeous illusions and reflections, possessing what Lawrence called "the sinister quality of an evil nightmare conjured by a mad prophet of Doomsday." When production began in Mexico in early 1946, aboard Errol Flynn's yacht (renamed *Circe* for shooting), there was no finished script and precious little advance planning. Both the characters and the plot were sketchy, as if imagined in a hallucination or interrupted dream. In postproduction, narration and newly shot close-ups would become essential to comprehending characters, motivations, and desire. The climactic scenes especially needed

bolstering to, in Lawrence's words, "show where Michael's nightmare left off and the Crazy House began."

Replying to a query in 1949 from critic Karel Reisz regarding her edit, Lawrence responded that while the film would have benefitted from more preparation, serendipity sometimes worked in Welles's favor. As the director showed in many of his films, he was unrivaled at conjuring up fascinating concepts and ideas, but ill-suited to the disciplined, efficient, and collaborative mode of Hollywood studio production. What's more, once he became impatient or bored he typically moved on and left others to finish his work, thereby sabotaging his own projects.

Lawrence said of Welles, "His personality leaves an imprint on everything he does—and I found his mistakes interesting and baffling—and enjoyed Welles's own amazement at the little happy accidents that occurred from time to time as the film started to take form." But his sometimes chaotic way of working and lack of collegiality meant that the editor was often left to her own devices, cutting with little guidance. Welles's cherished "serendipity" sometimes provided the road map to completion.

The creation of the Crazy House climax can be considered a metaphor for the entire production—filled with bravura moments but sprawling into indulgence and extravagance. In the narrative, it follows the Chinese theater scenes where, according to Lawrence, "each cut was timed with a click track to obtain a definite rhythm"—a rhythm that stops when Elsa (Hayworth) suddenly appears holding a torch. Lawrence knew that in Michael's hallucinatory state (the result of his swallowing Arthur Bannister's pills)

Everett Sloane's oily attorney Arthur Bannister meets his well-deserved end in the spectacular finale of the film, but not before delivering a kiss-off to his murderous wife: "You're gonna need a good lawyer."

Lawrence's inspired editing of *The Lady from Shanghai*'s climactic fun house sequence, demonstrating layered dissolves and dramatic character juxtapositions achieved through multiple fine grain copies of the original negative.

anything was possible, including a weird chase in which he is both pursuer and pursued, trapped in a waking nightmare that dissolves into delirium.

Welles obsessively committed himself to this subjective sequence, to the extent that he spent hours designing and painting the bizarre interior himself, outfitting it with dismembered mannequins, mutilated clown faces, and other ghoulish touches intended to metaphorically represent the mind of a man gone mad. Welles shot enough of this fun house footage to make a separate film, but much of it—beside inflating the climax to an unreasonable length—would never have passed muster with the Motion Picture Production Code. Lawrence needed to pare down the excess while maintaining Welles's essential vision.

As for the shootout, the mirror maze itself contained 2,912 square feet of glass, with 80 plate glass mirrors and 24 distorting mirrors, some two-way, with which Welles could reflect the disorientation and duplicity of the main characters. Both practical effects and multiple exposures were used during shooting and in postproduction, including the addition of "impossible" frames where one character's visage completely surrounded another.

Lawrence explained that "the mirror maze was cut so as to introduce [Bannister's] two canes with greatest surprise—and the gun fight was cut to get the most suspense . . . yet keeping Bannister's death to the last possible moment." She went on to say, "The cuts in this sequence were so short in many instances that fine grains [first-generation prints from the camera negative] had to be cut and a dupe negative made in order to make the double exposures possible."

Despite the director's derision, it's safe to say that Lawrence's visual savvy and deft touch resulted in this sequence—and the film as a whole—being lauded as one of the most distinctive and memorable in the director's oeuvre.

THREE YEARS LATER, Lawrence's multi-decade résumé and a good working relationship with iconoclastic director Nicholas Ray earned her the assignment of editing *In a Lonely Place*. It was her third job for Humphrey Bogart's Santana Productions (*Knock on Any Door* [1949] and *Tokyo Joe* [1949] being the others) and her second go-round with Ray. It was the type of project that appealed to Lawrence, one filled "with emotion, drama, human sympathies," as she related in a newspaper interview.

One of the best pictures ever made about Hollywood, *In a Lonely Place* features Bogart's most autobiographical role. Writer Dixon Steele is an intelligent, self-loathing, alcoholic loner with a vicious temper and resentful attitude who becomes implicated in a

> " The creation of the Crazy House climax can be considered a metaphor for the entire production—filled with bravura moments but sprawling into indulgence and extravagance.

Laurel Gray (Gloria Grahame) assists screenwriter Dixon Steele (Humphrey Bogart) with script preparation during their torrid romance in the iconic Hollywood noir *In a Lonely Place*. Courtesy of Mary Mallory

murder. Santana had purchased Dorothy B. Hughes's Edgar Award–winning 1947 novel of the same name, and hired writer Edmund H. North to adapt it.

North's reworking of the novel included changing the main character from a sociopathic World War II veteran to a brooding screenwriter on the back end of his career. Bogart hired Ray—his director on *Knock on Any Door*—because of his compassion for psychologically struggling characters. The men also shared suspicions about the shallowness of Hollywood. Ray was in his own psychological struggle during the production, as he and wife Gloria Grahame—playing Dix's lover, Laurel Gray—had separated and were living apart.

The film is fueled by emotion—not only the deep passion between Dix and Laurel, but in the psychotic flare-ups that bedevil Bogart's character. Lawrence clearly felt all of this, remarking to a newspaper that "most actors do their best work in close-ups . . . the greatest emotion for everyone is realized when they look straight into the actor's face, in his or her eyes. The eyes to me are everything." Her editing would emphasize this.

In the scene where Dix first professes his love for Laurel, much is revealed in close-ups. As Bogart leans in for a kiss, Grahame looks up at him with adoration as he gently caresses her face and neck—also a foreshadowing of sinister things to come. In the concluding scene, Lawrence again chooses close-ups to emphasize the characters' anguish, both when Dix's exoneration comes too late and Bogart's mournful eyes fill with sad resignation, and in the final close-up of a tearful Grahame, heartbroken as her once passionate lover walks out of her life.

Lawrence's later work in noir never matched these two exceptional films. She edited such relatively formulaic titles as *The Miami Story* (1954), *Tight Spot* (1955), and *Chicago Syndicate* (1955), as well as the aforementioned 3-D feature *Man in the Dark*. As the preeminent editor at Columbia, she cut the studio's first color film, *Cover Girl* (1944), its first Cinemascope film, *Three for the Show* (1955), as well as the Frank Sinatra musical *Pal Joey* (1957), which earned her one of the two Academy Award nominations in her career (1960's *Pepe* was the other). Lawrence survived a changing and difficult industry for women for almost fifty years, while her husband, Frank, retired in the late 1930s. Though he did cut such films as *Bulldog Drummond* (1929), *Nana* (1934), and the dramatic *Hell's Angels* (1930), Frank never received the attention or success of his talented wife.

Despite her reputation within the industry, and her contributions to two bona fide noir classics, Viola Lawrence's work as an editor has been sadly overlooked. That's partly due to her self-effacing reticence about speaking publicly and her commitment to supporting the director's vision, minus any flashy flourishes. While Welles enthusiasts will always disparage her work on *The Lady from Shanghai* as marring the master's vision, the truth is that she stitched the film together with painstaking care and craftsmanship. Lawrence's own dictum was that editors should provide the "dramatic form, pace, and polish" to hold films together—while leaving the defining theatrical moments to the director. As much as anything, that's what has also kept her creativity obscured from critical appraisal. ∎

THE RUINED FACES OF NOIR

By Stefen Styrsky

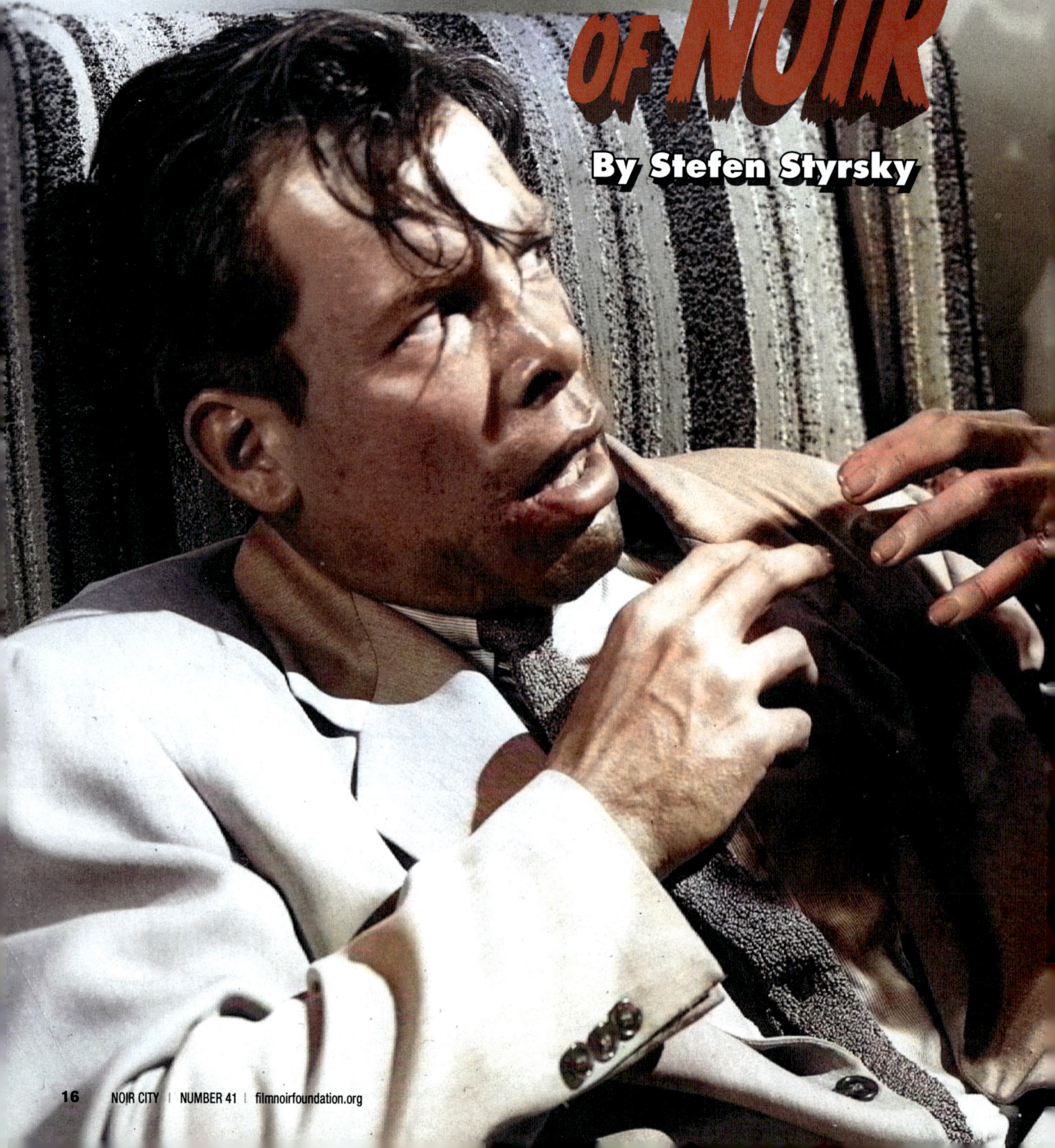

Few themes get to the heart of film noir like the double. From the cop moonlighting as a gangster to the housewife turned serial murderer, noir has always hinted that beneath the measured, smiling face a person lets the world see lives a shadow-self. One who might harbor delusional hopes, taboo desires, or murderous tendencies.

When this other person emerges—and in noir it always does—film demands some visual cue. A shift in lighting. A tilted frame. Different clothes. But a series of dark films also question the idea of a fixed personality through a much grimmer and more visceral adjustment: facial mutilation.

Based on a radio play, the script for *The Face Behind the Mask* was tailored to Peter Lorre, with future blacklistee Paul Jarrico probably shaping the film's scathing parody of the American dream.

The promise of lurid spectacle is a perennial draw for audiences, so body horror and the movies came up together: witness such silent and early sound films as *The Unknown* (1927), *The Man Who Laughs* (1928), and *Mad Love* (1935). During the classic noir era, it's easy to imagine the idea resonating as wounded servicemen began returning from Europe and the Pacific.

But facial-injury noir plays at more than shock value. While in the simplest view a scarred face can signal an inner corruption, these movies also explore how a changed appearance can be both freeing and damning. And all pose the troubling question: Who's really in there? The maimed faces of noir suggest that we harbor ideas, needs, and compulsions we can't, won't, or dare not look at.

THE FACE OF ANOTHER

On his first day in America, Hungarian immigrant Janos Szabo (Peter Lorre), the protagonist of *The Face Behind the Mask* (1941), is hideously burned in a fire

at his hotel. Before this, Janos is almost comically naive about his new country, and in the film's early moments it seems like America is truly a friendly and welcoming place, where even the cops—represented by the avuncular Lieutenant Jim O'Hara (Don Beddoe)—can spare a nickel for a new arrival.

But after Janos's face is melted, he discovers a second, dark-mirror nation, a callous double of the one reflected in the welcoming visage of Lady Liberty that the émigré so admired as his ship entered New York Harbor. On his arrival he quickly found employment, but after the fire his face is so repulsive no one will hire him for even the most basic manual labor. He's soon destitute and near suicide.

However, Janos also discovers a country ripe for plunder. Apparently, his former profession of watchmaker lends itself to carrying out the perfect crime. Tapping a harsh and pragmatic alter ego awakened by his injuries, Janos uses a horologist's patience and eye for detail

Lorre, who often enhanced his performances with facial scars, prosthetic teeth, or bald wigs, underwent his most dramatic transformation with help from makeup artist Ernie Parks in *The Face Behind the Mask*.

FROM M·G·M's HALL OF FAME
JOAN CRAWFORD

SCARFACED SHE-DEVIL!
"WHATEVER I AM— MEN MADE ME!"

in her most EXCITING *hit!* A **Woman's Face**

M-G-M'S ALL-TIME GREAT

with MELVYN DOUGLAS

Screen Play by DONALD OGDEN STEWART and ELLIOT PAUL · Directed by GEORGE CUKOR · Produced by VICTOR SAVILLE
AN M-G-M PICTURE

to lead a robbery gang on a spectacular series of heists.

Even though he steals to survive, Janos seesaws between embracing his new, harder personality and despising himself for succumbing to crime. This might be a case of protesting too much. Janos also seemingly has little compunction about spending the loot on clothes, cars, and houses. And the heists come off so easily that one wonders if behind the facade of a hard-working immigrant, part of him wasn't always on the make for an easy score.

The lifelike mask Janos eventually purchases to hide his scars further blurs the line between his personalities. (In this, the Hollywood B movie prefigures Hiroshi Teshigahara's existential horror film *The Face of Another* (1966), based on a novel by Kobo Abe about a disfigured chemical scientist.) Rather than pulling him toward his earlier self, the partial restoration of Janos's former appearance—represented by a coat of white paint and skin-tightening gauze that exaggerates the strangeness of Lorre's own face—only seems to hasten his moral decay. His cruelest and most calculating moments occur when he is wearing his mask.

FALSE FACES

The proposition that a scarred outcast has no choice but to resort to crime powers two other noirs.

In *A Woman's Face* (1941), a remake of the similarly titled Swedish film starring Ingrid Bergman, Joan Crawford plays Anna Holm. Horribly burned at the age of five when her drunken father set fire to the house, Anna now leads a criminal gang. Further proof that mob

> " Rather than returning him to his earlier self, the partial restoration of Janos's appearance only seems to hasten his moral decay. His cruelest and most calculating moments occur when he is wearing his mask.

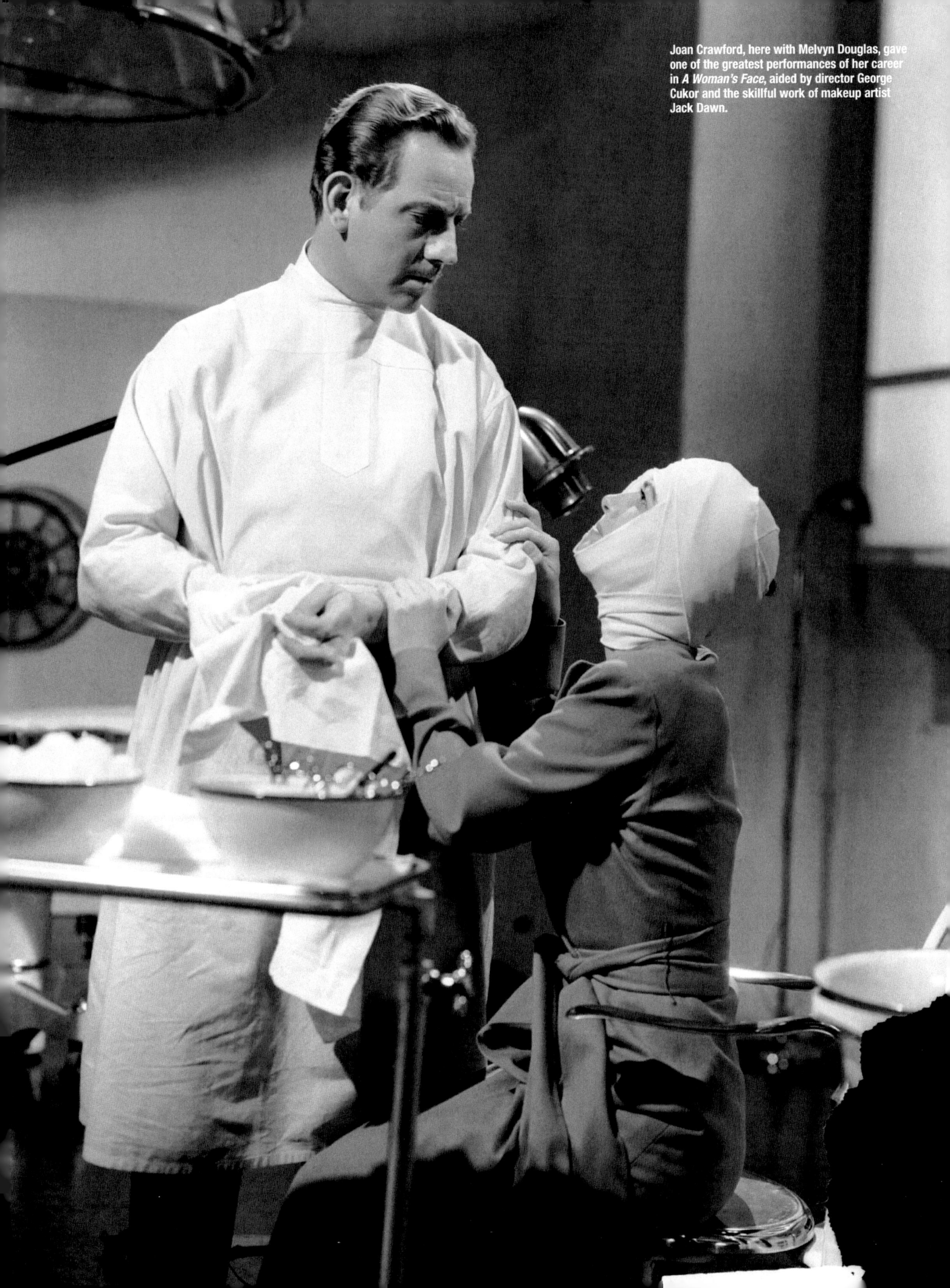

Stolen Face, starring Paul Henreid and Lizabeth Scott in a dual performance, was made by British director Terence Fisher for Hammer Films before his shift toward horror.

boss is seemingly a viable occupation for the disfigured in movies.

Unlike Janos, Anna arrives kiln-hardened. She disdains concepts such as love and empathy and revels in the damage she wreaks. Her wound is not only a physical injury but the sign of a marred soul. "The world was against me, so I'd be against the world," she says.

Enter the suave, unctuously charming Torsten Barring played by Conrad Veidt, who as the star of *The Man Who Laughs* was no stranger to facial-disfigurement cinema. Intrigued because the man doesn't flinch when he glimpses her scars, Anna falls into something like love, and goes along when Barring proposes they blackmail the adulterous Vera Segert (Osa Massen), wife of famous surgeon Gustaf Segert (Melvyn Douglas). Barring might not bear any visible marks, but Anna recognizes a fellow misanthrope when she sees one.

In a fateful twist, Dr. Segert happens to be a noted plastic surgeon. He takes pity on Anna's embittered criminality and offers to repair her face. He believes that once she's no longer an outcast her latent humanity will surface. As he says after the final operation (making a common mistake about the protagonist of Mary Shelley's novel) Anna is either his "Galatea or Frankenstein." Will Anna's appearance now unlock her repressed inner beauty, or has Segert created a femme fatale? The rest of the film holds a literal trial to answer the question.

In *Stolen Face* (1952), reconstructive surgeon Philip Ritter (Paul Henreid) believes that it's society's fault when disfigured men and women turn to crime. He specializes in repairing the faces of maimed criminals so that they have a chance at a normal life. His latest chal-

lenge is Lily Conover (Mary Mackenzie), a young woman facially scarred during the London Blitz. Her personality is as jagged as her cracked looks, a fact she's quick to blame on the scorn her injuries provoke. "Nobody wants someone like me around," she tells Ritter.

Unfortunately, Lily has fallen into the hands of a love-addled Pygmalion. Ritter not only sculpts Lily into the image of Alice Brent (Lizabeth Scott), the woman who rejected him for another man, but compounds the fiction by marrying new-Lily (played by Scott mouthing a cockney accent as contrived as the film's plot), and then, a la *Vertigo*, tries to refashion her in the classier image of his lost love.

Circumscribed as she was by injury and petty crime, Lily becomes a different type of captive, prisoner to Ritter's obsessive love for another woman. Her damaged face might signal a core amorality, but it's also a channel for Ritter's bent mind, allowing him to soothe his neurotic longings in the fantasy of the ideal woman.

While *A Woman's Face* and *Stolen Face* probe the way appearance is both truth and illusion, they dodge hard questions about society's superficiality, the hierarchy of beauty, and the primacy of male desire.

Anthony Mann takes a different approach to these themes in *Strange Impersonation* (1946). Brilliant research chemist Nora Goodrich (Brenda Marshall) has formulated a breakthrough anesthetic. In a rush to prove the chemical's efficacy, Nora tests the substance on herself, aided by her assistant, Arline Cole (Hillary Brooke). The experiment starts a fire and an unconscious Nora is powerless to stop it. She wakes in the hospital with a horribly burned face.

for a prominent scar on one cheek.

Muller sees this as the perfect opportunity to escape not only the hitmen gunning for him, but also the authorities who want him jailed for multiple parole violations. He slices his face in the same spot and then murders Bartok so that he can take the man's place.

Even though it's later revealed that Muller cut the wrong side of his face, the scheme comes off with surprising ease, perhaps because Bartok was as big a narcissist as Muller, only of a different flavor. Rather than disappearing behind a new identity, Muller has stepped into an alternate version of himself.

In a final irony, Bartok was deep in debt to gangsters who, looking for the doctor, kill Muller instead. An eleventh-hour change of heart, when Muller has softened enough to fall in love with Bartok's secretary, Evelyn Hahn (Joan Bennett), can't save him. His self-inflicted wound is no refuge, merely a transference of crime and guilt, the face of a marred inner personality he refused to probe.

Nora Prentiss (1947) has San Francisco cardiologist Richard Talbot (Kent Smith) enjoying the fruits of a well-tended life: flourishing practice, devoted wife, big house, well-adjusted children. Except he unconsciously loathes it all. The day-in day-out routine is crushing him. Rigid and proper even in the eyes of his peers, Talbot is drained of spontaneity and joy by his overly scheduled life of patient appointments, familial duty, and social calls.

It's inevitable that after a chance meeting with nightclub singer Nora Prentiss (Ann Sheridan), he blunders into an affair with her. But still beholden to his shell existence, he can't leave his wife or a career he no longer loves.

Fate intervenes when a male patient dies in Talbot's office. The doctor thinks nothing of planting evidence on the body to make it look like his own and sending the corpse in his own car over a

Adding to Nora's despair over her wounds and a foundering career, Arline conspires to keep her separated from her fiancé, Stephen Lindstrom (William Gargan). Once Nora and Stephen's estrangement is complete, Arline marries Stephen.

But a distraught and lonely Nora realizes that her face, now unrecognizable, is also a second chance. After a complicated sequence of events that end in Nora accidentally killing a woman trying to blackmail her, she assumes the dead woman's identity and heads to California. She hires a surgeon to rebuild her face—one of her own choosing—that she can use to restart her life.

While the film's brevity and cabinet-dregs cocktail of medical thriller, crime picture, and psychological melodrama blunts the theme, *Strange Impersonation* refuses to engage in a retread of "woman forged in man's image." Rather than allowing a man to dictate how she'll look and who she becomes, Nora chooses her own path. A wrecked face is the door to a fresh start.

THE MAN WITH THE GETAWAY FACE

But is a changed appearance really a second chance?

In *Hollow Triumph* (aka *The Scar*, 1948) career criminal John Muller (Paul Henreid) is on the run after the botched robbery of a mob-run casino. In the kind of twist that always seems perfectly mundane to those living in Dark City, Muller encounters psychiatrist Dr. Bartok, his exact double (even down to the accent!) except

"It's a bitter little world," as Joan Bennett tells Paul Henreid in *The Scar*, a B film with superb cinematography by John Alton and a clever script by Daniel Fuchs.

Kent Smith's straight-arrow doctor tells nightclub singer Ann Sheridan (the titular Nora Prentiss) that he's writing a paper on ailments of the heart. "A paper?" she quips, "I could write a book."

cliff. Then, Talbot uses the man's identity to flee to New York.

Except in noir, it's never that easy. Talbot is soon forced into hiding when his picture shows up in the papers because his "death" is being investigated as a homicide. Only after he emerges from a real car accident with a mug scorched to the consistency of melted rubber does he think he's free. But the smashup attracts the attention of the police, who arrest Talbot under his assumed identity as his killer. Unrecognizable beneath the scars, his new face has only bound him to his former self.

During the subsequent trial, the film keeps Talbot's injuries mostly hidden in shadow, rear profile shots, or at a distance. But with the echoing courtroom judgment of "guilty" comes a full-on closeup of Talbot's ruin. His disfigurement isn't the chance at a new life. Instead, it's the literal ugliness of a parallel self he'd never admit to har-

"I never felt better in my life," Glora Grahame's Debby Marsh says before dispensing justice from a loaded gun. Her boyfriend Lee Marvin is horrified by her new persona in *The Big Heat.*

Scripted by former crime reporter Sydney Boehm, *The Big Heat* was one of many films made in response to the 1951 Kefauver hearings into organized crime, which alerted people to the prevalence of civic corruption and racketeering. The film's brutal violence is all the more shocking for the fact that much of it is directed at women.

boring: his shoddy soul, his facility for lying, his many betrayals. As the physician says while scissoring away Talbot's bandages, "It's always a shock when you see yourself for the first time."

THE FACE IN THE MIRROR

The über-film of facial-injury noir is Fritz Lang's *The Big Heat* (1953), in which homicide detective Dave Bannion (Glenn Ford) sets out for revenge after witnessing his wife, Katie (Jocelyn Brando), blown up in a car bomb rigged for him.

It would be wrong to blame Bannion for the terrible event, but beneath the cool exterior on display when he's first introduced studying the scene of a fellow cop's suicide chafes an angry man. After receiving a threatening phone call meant to scare him off a murder case, the detective barges into mob boss Mike Lagana's (Alexander Scourby) mansion and returns the favor by roughing up a bodyguard. A more strategic guy might've realized this would imperil his family. The rogue-gun tactics only provoke Lagana and get Katie killed.

Bannion's angry man takes control after his wife's death. Furious when his corrupt superiors stonewall the case, and perhaps subconsciously guilt-wracked over the role (however inadvertent) he played in the tragedy, the detective goes off the rails. He turns in his badge and alienates his few cop friends. While conducting his own investigation, Bannion uses an elderly woman to lure a gangster into a trap, something his earlier self would likely peg a coward's move. Once a charmingly devoted father, he pawns his daughter off on relatives so he can hunt for his wife's killers, at first blind to how this places the girl in terrible danger. And out of sheer rage, Bannion almost compromises his principles by nearly murdering the corrupt wife of a crooked policeman.

Initially, good-time mob girl Debby Marsh (Gloria Grahame) seems to have nothing in common with the detective. She first appears draped on a couch like an odalisque, then taking a long look at herself in a full-length mirror. Later she's shown before the same mirror openly admiring her beauty, in another scene applying lipstick. The frequent doubling of her image is more than evidence of unchecked vanity. The shots hint that someone else prowls beneath Debby's fashion-model looks.

This person emerges after her mob-enforcer boyfriend, Vince (Lee Marvin), catches her lying about a (chaste) evening she spent with Bannion. Vince only knows the partial truth and, none too happy about what he believes is her two-timing, tosses a pot of boiling coffee into Debby's face.

When the bandages come off, Debby is a study in contrasts. A web of knotted scars cover half her face, the other half remains unmarred silk. And just as the car bomb propelled Bannion from dutiful cop to "hate binge" vigilante, Debby's wrecked beauty summons a woman angrier, more iron-willed than the sponging chippy whose strongest skill was pouring a martini. She allows this new self free reign, burning a path of not only revenge, but also justice, as she systematically dismantles the city's crime syndicate. Unlike Bannion's inner scars, Debby's injuries make her a better person.

When they meet again, Bannion glimpses in the unfortunate Debby the person he's become—pitiless, homicidal, and self-destructive. But only after she's fatally wounded during a shootout with Vince does he fully understand his dual and dueling selves. Unlike the doomed antiheroes in *Hollow Triumph* and *Nora Prentiss*, Bannion is saved by this moment of self-recognition, avoiding the path of self-destruction by instead choosing one of redemption. ■

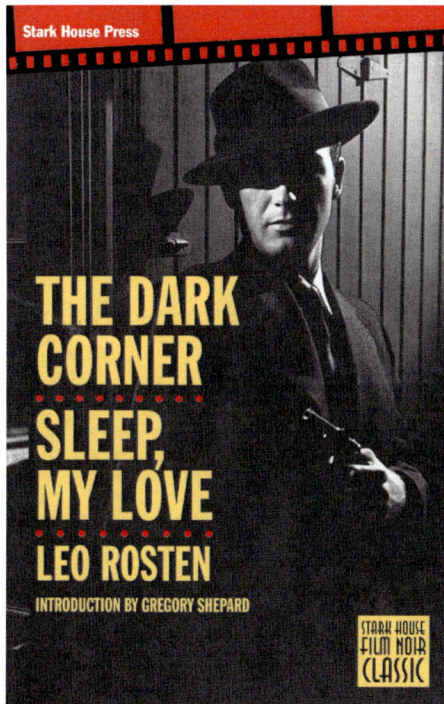

A POOR SUBSTITUTE
FOR WISDOM

Finger Man, a Forgotten Crime, and
the Impossible Hollywood Dream

By Jason A. Ney

"I put the finger on Public Enemy Number One!"

I n 1955, Allied Artists released one of its many late-cycle noirs, chock-full of the nastiness that audiences had come to expect from a film of its ilk: a hardened criminal-turned-informant, bloody fisti-cuffs, bullet-riddled bodies, and heaping helpings of misogyny. *Finger Man* stars Frank Lovejoy, no stranger to tough-guy roles, as crooked loner Casey Martin, arrested and press-ganged by the cops into turning against the only kind of man he's ever been. While fictionalized, the story had been ripped from the headlines, adapted from the life story of a man whose background had "film noir" written all over it.

The Dickensian childhood Morris Lipsius spent in New York's Lower East Side featured a father wracked by tuberculosis and stuck in a hospital, along with an exhausted, impoverished mother hemmed in by five children, needing to throw something—or someone—overboard to stay afloat. Morris drew the short straw, got bounced into a Hebrew orphanage, then bounced himself out at age thirteen, ending his formal education.

When he hit the streets in 1927, during the heady days of Prohibition's bootlegging boom, there was no shortage of off-the-books opportunities to learn the dark arts of criminal enterprise. He did side gigs for mob bosses, but his main gigs—cowboying* and moll buzzing*—he kept for himself. The cops popped him for a purse snatching gone sideways not long after he turned eighteen, and the judge sent him packing to the New York City reformatory for ten months

to cool his heels. When he got out, he went right back to stick-up jobs, until one shop owner took advantage of his diminutive stature by wrapping him in a bear hug until the cops arrived. No monthslong sentence this time: the judge decided that Lipsius would benefit from a lengthier sentence—seven and a half to fifteen years—to properly learn remorse. He began serving his time at Sing Sing but transferred to Great Meadow, where he rubbed shoulders with Lucky Luciano and befriended another fellow inmate named Frank O'Leary.

You want to get out early? O'Leary asked him. *Ditch the tall tale you've been telling the parole board and be more truthful.* It worked. But four years of freedom ended in an instant once Lipsius got busted for running numbers out of a candy store. Back to Great Meadow, stuck serving the entirety of his original sentence.

At some point, as part of a routine procedure, the prison staff tested his IQ. Lipsius's score came back preposterously high. They demanded a retest, which confirmed his off-the-charts book smarts. While they were probably asking themselves how such a smart guy could be so stupid, Rabbi Hyman E. Goldin, a prison chaplain, saw untapped potential. He hired Lipsius as his secretary and started pitching him and O'Leary on a project: a dictionary of gangster vernacular that the three men would edit together. Behind prison walls they hammered it out, and by the time the H. L. Mencken–endorsed *Dictionary of American Underworld Lingo* landed in bookstores in 1950, Lipsius was once again breathing free air, ready to go straight.

Back when Lipsius had been just a teenage hotshot, Waxey Gordon, another product of the Lower East Side, had been working hard at developing a resumé as a major player in the East Coast bootlegging racket. But once Luciano turned stoolie* on him, the government pulled a page from the Capone prosecution playbook, nabbing Gordon for tax evasion in 1933. After his release from prison in the early 1940s, he struck out for the West Coast, looking for new ways to collect ill-gotten gains. His black-market sugar operation landed him back behind bars for another year, and then, free for the second time, he started hocking heroin, which would turn into a booming national business by the 1950s.

In 1950, the government's narcotics bureau wanted to head that development off at the pass. Their yearslong investigation into Gordon's network hadn't yielded the kind of evidence they needed for a surefire conviction, so they sought out an inside man who could finger*

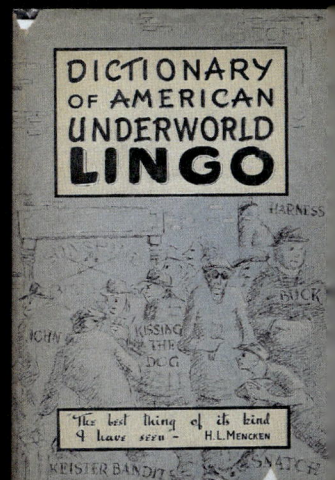

Morris Lipsius (seated) and Frank O'Leary, all smiles during the press blitz for the *Dictionary of American Underworld Lingo*.

" On the surface, Lipsius seemed to be turning into a productive member of society, and in retrospect, his shot at the big brass ring seemed a foregone conclusion.

In the 1950s, John Lardner enjoyed not only enormous popularity among the reading public, with a weekly sports-focused column in *Newsweek* and regular contributions to the *New Yorker*, but also universal respect among his peers. While he's mostly forgotten today, if a Mount Rushmore of sportswriters existed, his face would adorn it. He did, it should be noted, descend from writing royalty. His father, Ring Lardner, was the most well-known newspaper columnist during the Roaring Twenties, and counted F. Scott Fitzgerald and H. L. Mencken among his friends. (Producer Stanley Kramer adapted Ring Sr.'s short story "Champion" into the 1949 boxing noir that made Kirk Douglas a star.) John inherited his father's liter-

In addition to inspiring the character of Dutch Becker in *Finger Man*, fictionalized versions of Waxey Gordon have appeared on the shows *The Untouchables*, *The Lawless Years*, and *Boardwalk Empire*.

Gordon for the crime. Since Lipsius was again in danger of getting sent back to the slammer for bootlegging booze, would he be willing to set up Gordon in exchange for the government dropping his upcoming prosecution? The question practically answered itself.

Lipsius spent several months stalking Gordon's haunts, sidling up next to him at bars while he drank, listening to the gangster's stories of the good old days, and earning his trust. Then, on July 16, 1951, Lipsius put the first stage of the agents' plan into action. After a couple of preliminary buys to establish Gordon's bona-fides as a dope peddler, he and the cops laid the final trap. On August 2, while Gordon was walking across the street toward Lipsius, a package of junk* in hand, narcotics agents nabbed him.

In short order, Morris Lipsius became known as the man who took down Waxey Gordon. He penned a December 1952 cover story for *The Saturday Evening Post* ("I Put the Finger on Waxey Gordon") and a syndicated newspaper article titled "Three Theories in Slaying Case: Ex-Convict Gives Views on Slaying of Finger Man." For a time, he also traveled the country, giving public talks about the danger of heroin. On the surface, he seemed to be turning into a productive member of society, and in retrospect, his shot at the big brass ring seemed a foregone conclusion. But just exactly how *Finger Man* came together remains ripe for conjecture.

ary skills, as did his younger brother, Ring Jr., who worked primarily as a screenwriter, winning an Oscar for cowriting *Woman of the Year* (1942) and contributing to the noirs *Laura* (1944), *Cloak and Dagger* (1946), and *The Brasher Doubloon* (1947).

One of John's most memorable non-sports columns arrived in the December 1, 1951, issue of the *New Yorker*. "The Lexicographers in Stir" profiles the backgrounds of the three men who put together the *Dictionary of American Underworld Lingo*, which led to a collaboration with Lipsius on fashioning of the Lipsius/Gordon tale into the story for *Finger Man*.

Or did it?

In 1947, during the early days of the Red Scare, Ring Jr.'s outspoken views had landed him in hot water with the House Un-American Activities Committee, which subpoenaed him and nine other members of the filmmaking community, all either present or former Communists. The committee asked them, "Are you now or have you ever been a member of the Community party?" Ring Jr.'s response became the stuff of legend. He told J. Parnell Thomas, the New Jersey congressman who put the question to him, "I could answer it, but if I did, I would hate myself in the morning." Thomas kicked him out of the hearing. He and the other nine who refused to cooperate, citing their First Amendment rights, were found in contempt of Congress, sent off to prison, and branded as the Hollywood Ten. (Ring Jr. and Thomas once again crossed paths, this time in prison. The New Jersey pol had been convicted of inventing government employees who didn't exist and funneling their pay to himself.) Once Ring Jr. was released, he found himself blacklisted. Since no studio would touch the Ten, they wrote under pseudonyms or passed their scripts off to others who fronted their work for them.

Ring Jr. wrote in his memoir, *The Lardners: My Family Remembered*, that "John had no background in movies except as a critic." Conversely, Ring Jr. boasted a lengthy list of credits, not to mention an Academy Award. Did John really help Morris Lipsius fictionalize his own story? Or did Ring Jr. do the actual work of molding the story into shape before John pitched it to Hollywood studios under his name? Strange bedfellows, either way.

Regardless of which Lardner worked with Lipsius, the story in *The Saturday Evening Post* gained such traction that in early 1954, gossip columnist Louella Parsons claimed to have recently read it during a flight, and "it held me so completely engrossed that we had landed before I was conscious that we were home." As she reported, producer Lindsley Parsons, a long-time collaborator with Monogram-turned-Allied Artists, had recently optioned the *Post* story from Lipsius, who had "been living under an assumed name and hiding out from possible mob violence ever since the article was printed. Only the FBI knows his whereabouts—one of their top secrets."

But by January 1955, when the film began production, the gangster-turned-informant decided to risk public exposure by making his way to Hollywood. As the film shot in such notable Los Angeles locales as Griffith Park and Skid Row, Lipsius served as its technical advisor, energetically running around the set and helping

fake gangsters act more like the real thing.

While no classic, *Finger Man* sits comfortably among the better half of the increasingly brutal, no-nonsense noirs of the mid to late 1950s. Lovejoy finds the humanity in what could have become a one-note character; Peggie Castle locates the tragic loneliness of the doomed Gladys; and Timothy Carey exploits his trademark twitchiness to steal every scene in which he appears as blustery, pathetic henchman Lou. Director Harold D. Schuster and cinematographer William A. Sickner—both fresh from the solid noir *Loophole* (1954)—bring the typical level of competent professionalism that kept men like them employed during the dying days of the studio system.

For Lipsius, the film's relative merits probably mattered less than

From the *Dictionary of American Underworld Lingo*

Cowboy, n. A thief who operates in Wild West tradition; a reckless thief; a thief who flourishes weapons or assaults victims unnecessarily. "Them lousy cowboys, only punk kids breaking their cherry (operating for the first time) on the heist (holdup), burned up (overworked) this town."

Finger, n. 1. (Comparatively rare) A plainclothesman disguised as a member of the underworld. 2. A stoolpigeon, especially an underworld member, who buys police immunity in exchange for valuable information; an informer. 3. One who points out victims to a hired killer, thief, or terrorist; the act of pointing out the intended victim. 4. The act of pointing out, naming, or revealing the whereabouts of one wanted by the police; formal identification of a suspect in the police lineup or court. "If it wasn't for a finger, I'd never fall (be arrested) on this rap (charge)."

Finger, v. 1. To point out, name, or reveal the whereabouts of one wanted by the police; to make a formal identification of a suspect in a police lineup or in court. "The rapper (complainant) made (recognized) me and fingered me, so I grabbed a plea (pleaded guilty to a lesser offense)." 2. To point out a victim to a hired killer, a terrorist, thieves, etc. "That the geepo (rat) that fingered Dutch when he got hit in the noggin (shot to death). He catch slugs (be murdered) himself yet."

Junk, n. 1. Narcotics; drugs. "That junk pushing (selling) grift (racket) is a creep's (unprincipled fellow's) racket." 2. Any cheap imitation, such as imitation jewelry; a **stiff**. 3. Any stolen goods other than cash, especially jewelry.

Moll-buzz, n. A technique of snatching women's purses from baby carriages. [Note: The theft is accomplished in the following manner: An accomplice, known as the **buzzer**, accosts a victim and asks to be directed to a given place in the neighborhood. The destination is so chosen that the victim must turn her back to the carriage to point. The purse-snatcher now advances from the direction that the victim is facing and deftly seizes the purse. The victim seldom discovers her loss until the thieves have disappeared. Premature discovery requires the **buzzer**, feigning solicitude, to block pursuit and delay any outcry until the snatcher has escaped. Very youthful operators are most successful. There are several variations of this technique. Sometimes a second accomplice is used, a boy who sells paper market-bags. He and the snatcher converge on the baby carriage from opposite directions so that the seized purse may be swiftly dropped into an open market-bag. Arrests in this form of thievery are infrequent, and the thief is rarely found in possession of the stolen purse.]

Peep, v. To betray associates; to give information to the police.

Stool or Stoolie, n. An informer; a stool pigeon.

Stool pigeon, n. One who barters underworld secrets for immunity from police interference in petty rackets. [Note: In the strict sense of the term, a stool pigeon is not, as is generally supposed, one who informs under extreme police pressure; he is not a casual informer.]

As he so often did, Timothy Carey (right, holding a rod) brought hefty doses of oddball sleaze to his performance in *Finger Man*, opposite Frank Lovejoy.

seeing his name up on the big screen in the credits and witnessing Casey Martin, his filmic stand-in, transform from cynical criminal to government informant to self-sacrificing crusader. The film's tidy repackaging of his life as a tale of brutal redemption reaches its climax as Martin takes down vicious racketeer Dutch Becker (Forrest Tucker) and tells the audience via voiceover, "I know that I want to make something of my life. I'm going to try. I hope I live long enough to prove it."

On May 23, 1966, in a room at the Wagon Wheel Motel in Santa Ana, California, William Wayne Wagner pulled out a .45 and shot Lipsius seven times, killing him.

In the immediate aftermath of the shooting, Wagner told the *Independent Press-Telegram* (Long Beach, CA) that back in 1953, when he was just a teenager earning a living as a boxer in Canton, Ohio, he had met a gambler named Morris who bet on his fights, won some money, and thanked Wagner by buying him a boxing robe and paying off some of his small debts. Within a matter of months, Wagner went into the Army, causing them to lose touch, but after he got out of the service and settled in El Monte, California, he unwittingly met Lipsius's nineteen-year-old daughter, Linda. When he gave her a ride home from the horse stables where he was working, the two men met again and got to talking. Lipsius revealed that after spending his windfall from *Finger Man*, he'd kept

the money flowing by becoming a hit man.

During their conversation, Lipsius also outlined his plans to set up another Murder, Inc., modeled on the notorious Great Depression–era murder-for-hire outfit tied to Lucky Luciano. In his telling, a client had recently paid him $160 to murder a man. Lipsius avoided saying too much, such as the man's name (later identified as Michael McDonagh), or that he'd committed the murder in Lipsius's own shop, Otto's Food Store. (The police would later arrest Lipsius's daughter and son, believing they had helped him drag McDonagh's body into the alley when he couldn't do it himself, then aided in cleaning up McDonagh's blood. They were eventually released due to lack of evidence.) However, the police believed this wasn't a hit at all, but a robbery—that Lipsius had murdered one of his regular customers and stolen the alleged payoff from McDonagh's body.

Each successive revelation about Lipsius's murder sent the case spiraling further into chaos, with a twist-laden chronology that rivals the most convoluted noir thrillers. When the police arrived at the Wagon Wheel, they found not one dead man, but two: Lipsius and another man named Donald MacMillan. Initially, Wagner insisted he'd shot Lipsius in self-defense after Lipsius had shot and killed MacMillan after a night of drinking. Only one problem: Lipsius had fired a .25 caliber handgun, and the autopsy revealed Wagner's .45 had been used to kill both men. After the police arrested him for murder, Wagner kept peeling the onion, revealing that he had actually been working undercover to help the police nab Lipsius for McDonagh's murder. He also claimed he had been working as a police informant for years.

When Lipsius had told Wagner about murdering McDonagh, Wagner said he'd gone to the police, and that the LA cops asked him to get more information about it so they could make an arrest. In his version, Lipsius had showed up at his car agency, they'd gone for a drink, and a highly agitated Lipsius had asked to borrow money. Sensing danger, Wagner went home, picked up his .25, and made a call to the police to peep* on Lipsius.

Once Wagner returned with his gun, MacMillan joined them and supposedly chattered on about his bundle of money. When he invited the two men back to his hotel room, Lipsius grabbed the .25 from Wagner's pocket. At that point, Wagner says he made up a reason to go home again to get his .45. He tried to convince Lipsius to leave with him, to no avail. Wagner left by himself, got his second gun, and hoofed it back to the hotel room, where MacMillan—who

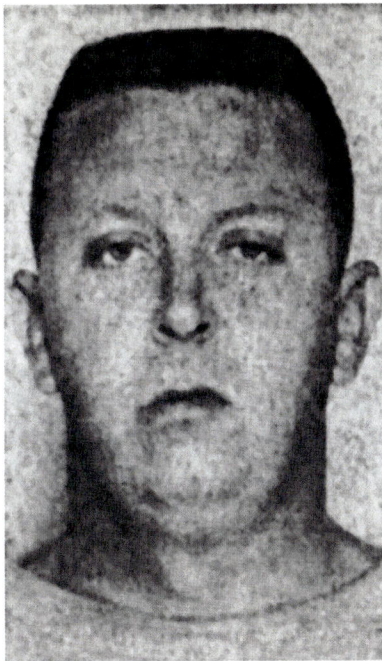
William Wayne Wagner's mugshot

worked as a job counselor—was sitting in a chair with some papers, talking about potential work for Lipsius, who was standing behind him. When Lipsius pulled out Wagner's .25 and pointed it at MacMillan's head, Wagner said, "I got scared. I waited for the police to jump in and break it up. I thought they were watching through the window. I didn't know then that they hadn't arrived. Nothing happened, and I pulled my gun and fired."

He thought he'd only hit Lipsius, not realizing until later that MacMillan had also been shot, which he attributed to Lipsius. Once the police arrived, Wagner gave his statement, went to breakfast with one of the detectives, and then went to work. His freedom lasted all of two hours before the autopsy results came back. The police arrested him, a grand jury heard the evidence and declined to indict him, and the DA dismissed the charges. When reflecting on the outcome, Wagner said, "I don't regret killing Lipsius. I knew what I was doing. But there is no way I can ever make up for shooting MacMillan. That is the real tragedy."

> " By 1966, *Finger Man* had already fallen into obscurity. As the media hustled toward the next tragedy, the tragic real-life tale of Morris Lipsius was likewise forgotten.

Even now, several details about the killings remain maddeningly opaque, like figures in outline, moving silently through the fog. Why did, as one local newspaper reported, the LA police believe Wagner owed Lipsius $4,000? And what of the witnesses who claimed that MacMillan hadn't spent the evening drinking with the two men, but instead spent all of it—save twenty minutes—in the Wagon Wheel's lobby, watching television? On the other hand, why did the police's story about their relationship with Wagner shift more than once? After initially denying they had ever employed Wagner in any capacity, they eventually admitted that he had done some work for them as a "volunteer secret associate." During the three days of grand jury testimony, the Santa Ana police chief also claimed that they had never issued a badge or a police ID card to Wagner, but then backtracked when evidence showed the opposite.

Wagner sued the police more than once, seeking $165,000 for wrongful arrest and $5,000 for breach of oral contract. According to available evidence, neither suit went anywhere, with the latter somehow getting tossed from court at least four times. By 1966, *Finger Man* had already fallen into obscurity. As the media hustled toward the next tragedy, the tragic real-life tale of Morris Lipsius was likewise forgotten.

Finger Man's appeal stems from its sympathetic portrayal of characters hanging on to the fringes of respectable society. They want to go straight but struggle to conquer the demons that keep dragging them back into the darkness. Many of them don't survive, but Casey Martin claws his way toward an aspirational ending, believing that he has found a way of living a more stable and fulfilling life. It's a nice thought. And one that, for Lipsius, proved utterly unattainable. His intelligence, no matter how impressive, was a poor substitute for the hard-won wisdom Martin gains by the time the credits roll. Morris Lipsius simply couldn't live up to the silver screen version of himself. How could anyone? ■

THE AUDACITY OF CRUISING

Forty-Four Years Later, Friedkin's Cop Noir Is Still Controversial, Misunderstood, and Disturbing

By Carsten Andresen

William Friedkin's police procedural *Cruising* (1980) was a groundbreaking release. While virtually every previous cop movie portrayed gay men as marginal and/or comedic, *Cruising* radically departed from heteronormative convention by focusing on a gay subculture of bondage, discipline, dominance, and sadomasochism (BDSM). The director conducted extensive research for *Cruising* and, being the committed filmmaker he was, would often visit BDSM clubs in nothing more than a jockstrap. These visits inspired him to recreate scenes of man-on-man kissing, groping, nipple play, fellatio, fisting, and golden showers. Nothing was off limits.

Film scholar D. A. Miller, commenting on *Cruising*'s verisimilitude, recognized that the director was "openly . . . [and] . . . keenly curious about radical gay sexual practice" and that this "curiosity visibly—ineffaceably—structures his film." This approach did not prove popular. Friedkin's evocation of this demimonde was so explicit that the Motion Picture Association continued to complain of X-rated content even after he cut forty minutes and obscured certain images to secure an R rating. Some theater chains followed suit and refused to screen even the "censored" version over fears of negative press. The film's audacity doomed it in the short term, but it also ensured, over time, its singular legacy.

Cruising follows an NYPD officer who, seeking a promotion to detective, goes undercover to solve a series of murders targeting gay men. Gay activists of the time accused the film of sensationalizing homophobic violence and depicting gay men as sexual outlaws. What Friedkin was really attempting was the reengineering of the traditional police procedural to expose the dangers the gay community faced in the United States. In a prescient 1979 editorial, gay novelist John Rechy spotlighted how *Cruising* had the potential to illuminate "the troubling subject of violence toward" gay men that was "virtu-

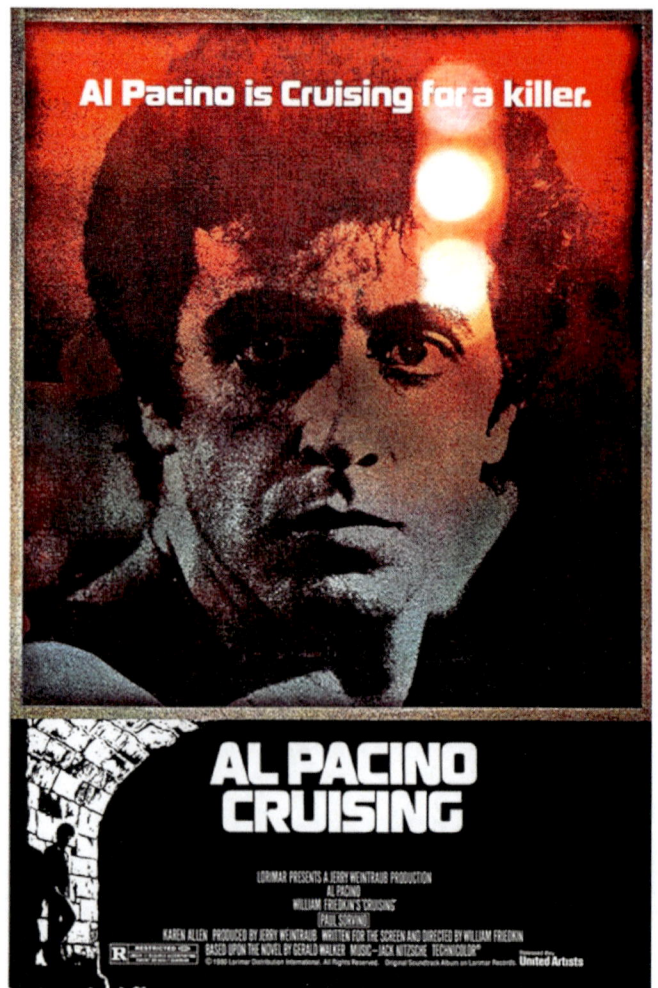

Al Pacino is Cruising for a killer.

AL PACINO CRUISING

LORIMAR PRESENTS A JERRY WEINTRAUB PRODUCTION AL PACINO WILLIAM FRIEDKIN'S CRUISING PAUL SORVINO KAREN ALLEN PRODUCED BY JERRY WEINTRAUB WRITTEN FOR THE SCREEN AND DIRECTED BY WILLIAM FRIEDKIN BASED UPON THE NOVEL BY GERALD WALKER MUSIC—JACK NITZSCHE TECHNICOLOR® R RESTRICTED ©1980 Lorimar Distribution International. All Rights Reserved. Original Soundtrack Album on Lorimar Records. Distributed thru United Artists

William Friedkin regretted his decision to cast Al Pacino after his first choice, Richard Gere, passed, but he eventually warmed to Pacino's tense lead performance.

ally unknown" to people beyond "the victims of that violence." The film also chastises the police for their failure to prioritize the safety of the LGBTQ+ community.

In bringing *Cruising* to the screen, Friedkin scrapped most of Gerald Walker's 1970 source novel and wrote a new script—his first—based on a series of gay homicides that had occurred in Manhattan. The director's interest stemmed from a personal acquaintance. In the late 1970s, he learned that police had arrested Paul Bateson, a bit player in the director's horror masterpiece *The Exorcist* (1973), for the murder of film journalist Addison Verrill. Friedkin, whose debut feature was a documentary about an inmate on death row, rushed to Rikers Island to meet with Bateson. According to the director, Bateson said the police were promising him a lenient sentence if he pleaded guilty to the murders of multiple gay men. Bateson's case, coupled with articles penned by *Village Voice* journalist Arthur Bell, spurred Friedkin to hire two former New York City police detectives—Randy Jurgensen and Sonny Grosso—as consultants. The director was striving for authenticity on all fronts, and would subsequently cast his consultants as (what else?) cops in the film.

Friedkin derived his narrative from an assignment that Jurgensen had accepted in the 1960s. The detective posed as a gay man to solve several crimes—robbery, extortion, and murder—that had been targeting gay victims. In *Cruising*, Captain Edelson (Paul Sorvino) orders officer Steve Burns (Al Pacino) to move into a new apartment for an off-the-books investigation. Burns rents the place

using an alias and gives up the two most prominent emblems of his police identity—his badge and gun. The young officer is also forbidden from telling Nancy Gates (Karen Allen), whom he's living with, about his undercover assignment.

Cruising recalls earlier film noirs such as *T-Men* (1947) and *Border Incident* (1949) that feature undercover officers inserting themselves into an underworld milieu. However, *Cruising* subverts the traditional masculinity of such scripts by having Burns posing as a Mata Hari–like honey trap, a role traditionally occupied by women in classics like *Notorious* (1946) and *Lured* (1947) and contemporary releases like *Black Widow* (1987) and *Impulse* (1990). As in undercover tales featuring female protagonists, Burns is bombarded with sexually aggressive advances from men. He carries this aggression over to his personal life. Burns's attempts to assert his heterosexuality backfire, however, when Nancy becomes exasperated by his secretiveness and decides she needs a break from their relationship.

Obsessive detectives are mainstays of police procedurals. Like those in Friedkin's *The French Connection* (1971) and *To Live and Die in L.A.* (1985), Burns turns amoral in his commitment to solving the case. He visits leather bars by night and, with seemingly little discomfort, acclimates to "playing" gay. By day, he befriends a neighbor who is gay, and becomes increasingly invested in the man's unhealthy relationship with his boyfriend. Are Burns's actions part of his undercover role—or a gradual revelation of his true self? Friedkin leaves the question open-ended, which emphasizes the film's morally ambiguous approach to both sexuality and violence.

Friedkin (right) weaves a tangled web around his star. He never told Pacino whether or not his character was a killer.

The viewer is never told how or what to think, because Burns is never quite sure himself.

Cruising also incorporates what filmmaker-critic Paul Schrader calls the "opposite principle." The film challenges the iconography of the blue uniform as an embodiment of law and order. In the first appearance of the police, a medical examiner shows an unkempt detective the severed arm of a male homicide victim. The detective declines to investigate, citing: "Circumstances undetermined pending police investigation." The medical examiner, taken aback, grumbles, "It's just a numbers game to you guys." In the next scene, two uniformed officers in a prowl car detain a pair of trans women. Rather than questioning them about the murders, the cops shake the women down for sex. Later, in a moment of visual genius, a group of uniformed police officers, indistinguishable from the NYPD, are revealed to be gay men dancing in a leather bar. It's here that *Cruising* reveals itself to also be an exploration of two (primarily) male fraternities.

Walker's novel portrayed gay men as effeminate scavengers seeking anonymous sex in public. But the film, released a year before the first AIDS case was identified in the United States, captures a period in Manhattan when men confidently pursued sexual freedom despite criminal repercussions. *Cruising* also pushed boundaries by recruiting real leather bar patrons as extras. The casualness is unmistakable. Friedkin's camera stalks through barely lit bar interiors, at every turn catching glimpses of unsimulated consensual sex between non-actors. *Cruising* is one of the first major studio releases to depict this side of out-and-proud gay life, which is presented as a protective, tight-knit community. Tellingly, the victims only face violence when they leave the sanctity of their BDSM bubble.

Like *He Walked by Night* (1948), *Cruising* features a paternal police captain shepherding a protégé through an investiga-tion's mental and physical rigors. Instructed by Friedkin to play a mid-level administrator who has witnessed the worst of humanity during his tenure, Sorvino gives an excellent performance as Captain Edelson. He is first seen in the morgue—eyes wide and clutching a handkerchief against his nose and mouth as he stares horrified at the brutalized body of a gay victim. He struggles to maintain his professionalism and steady his voice as he questions the medical examiner. In a film that interrogates authority and patriarchy, Edelson—who excels at the interpersonal aspects of homicide investigation—is presented as a humane and pragmatic father figure. He is not, however, the consistently moral police captain of noirs past.

When the investigation fails to net a viable suspect, Edelson faces the threat of termination. Under pressure, he sets aside his scruples and activates a reckless sting operation that culminates in his men torturing an innocent suspect. In a stunning scene, a Black police officer, carrying a whip and wearing only sunglasses, a jockstrap, and boots, struts up to a detained suspect and knocks him onto the floor. Terrified and confused, the suspect screams, "What are you doing to me?! Who is that guy?!" The scene is based on real NYPD tactics described by Jurgensen, and would go on to inspire photographer Robert Mapplethorpe's controversial images of African American model Ken Moody.

Cruising may present a fact-based and authentic-feeling police procedural, but the mystery of the killer's identity remains unclear. Is it Stuart Richards (Richard Cox), a Columbia graduate student haunted by the apparition of his deceased, homophobic father? Are there multiple killers? Is Burns one of them? To complicate the answer further, Friedkin cast multiple actors who closely resemble Richards—pale, dark curly hair, sunglasses, leather—to portray the

> **"** *Cruising* also incorporates what filmmaker-critic Paul Schrader calls the 'opposite principle.' The film challenges the iconography of the blue uniform as an embodiment of law and order.

The dark and the light: Stuart Richards (Richard Cox) perpetrates his crimes by night, while living a seemingly normal life by day.

Cruising sparked numerous protests due its lurid subject matter and perceived stigmatization of the LGBTQ community. A disclaimer stating otherwise was added to the opening credits.

killer (or killers). Unlike other directors, who cast different actors as red herrings to misdirect the audience, Friedkin pointedly calls out this convention by recasting actors who, earlier in the film, portrayed murder victims.

As in a horror film, these victims seemingly rise again to kill, like vampires. Friedkin also implies a kind of "demonic" possession, as the voice of each killer is overdubbed with that of Richards's father. In presenting a single paternal voice speaking through (and guiding) a hive mind of killers, *Cruising*—in technique and theme—evokes the twisted parentage in *Psycho* (1960) as well as predicting the homicidal patriarchy of *Twin Peaks* (1990–91). Richards is arrested and interrogated in the final act. He denies the killings while speaking in his father's voice, teasing—a la *Psycho*—a neat resolution to a messy case. Burns even gets promoted to detective. The film's noir ethos, however, ensures that this relief is short-lived.

Cruising refuses to compartmentalize the problem of homophobic violence, despite the police having "solved" the case. The film's penultimate scene sees Captain Edelson investigating a new murder— the brutal stabbing of Burns's gay neighbor. The film then cuts to a leather-clad figure, a Richards doppelganger, entering a leather bar— suggesting that a killer is still on the prowl. Friedkin then hits viewers with a mirror image of the film's opening shot—the Hudson River, from where the severed arm of the first victim was retrieved. While traditional police procedurals suggest that police restore order to society, this sequence eerily evokes the killer that would soon decimate a generation of gay men in the 1980s and 1990s—HIV/AIDS.

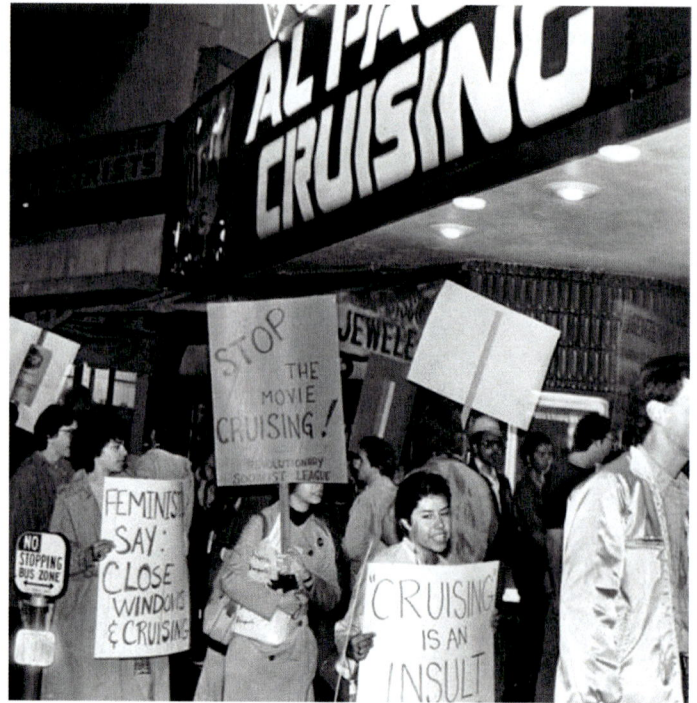

The film also deprives Burns of an emotional climax, which is fitting given the hours of unconsummated foreplay he engaged in while undercover. In the final scene, he promises to explain everything to Nancy after stopping by his apartment for a shave. Burns gazes into the bathroom mirror, contemplating his dual identities. Such a moment would typically signal a return to normalcy (i.e., the restorative love of an adoring woman), but Friedkin chooses to shift attention from Burns to Nancy. She finds her boyfriend's undercover BDSM outfit—mirrored sunglasses, leather aviator cap, leather jacket—and dons them to pose seductively. Burn's reaction to this provocative version of Nancy remains opaque. We only see him from Nancy's point of view, staring at her, expressionless. Whatever comes next, it feels ominous. When asked about his decision to break the fourth wall by having Burns look directly into the camera, Friedkin responded with a rhetorical question: "When you look at someone, do you really know who they are? . . . And who are you?" Burns may not yet have answers, but he knows he'll never be the same.

Cruising has been influential in multiple mediums. Burns was a reference point for closeted cop Danny Hawkins in James Ellroy's novel *The Big Nowhere* (1988), and *American Horror Story: NYC* (2022) reimagined the film's investigation as a ten-episode season of television. As a cinematic exploration of a specific gay subculture, however, *Cruising* has yet to be rivaled. It's hard to imagine it ever will. At least, not with an A-list star and Oscar-winning director attached. The film's unflinching depiction of BDSM and leather bars is just as controversial as it was during its initial release, and its insecure, sexually conflicted protagonist seems antiquated opposite the prouder, primarily female characters who have driven acclaimed queer noirs like *Bound* (1996) and *Love Lies Bleeding* (2024). Plot holes be damned, *Cruising* is the rare Hollywood release that's actually as transgressive, shocking, and daring as it claims to be. It's worth remembering, even if it still proves difficult to watch. ■

NOIR CITY
HEADSHRINKERS
PSYCHIATRISTS AS VILLAINS, ON-SCREEN AND OFF
NOIR CITY
ACTOR TO ACTOR
DANA DELANY ON GLORIA GRAHAME
LAVENDER NOIR
S.A. COSBY ON POINT BLANK
NOIR CITY
MODERN NOIR MASTER
MIKE HODGES
NOIR CITY
ONE HUNDRED YEARS OF JEAN-PIERRE MELVILLE
LINDA DARNELL'S DARK DESTINY
THE FATHER OF EUROPEAN NOIR
WINDRUSH NOIR
NOIR CITY
ELLROY Confidential
Modern Noir Master
THE FUGITIVE: THE DEFINITIVE NOIR SERIES
NOIR CITY
NOIR CITY
A FILM NOIR FOUNDATION PUBLICATION
NOIR CITY
DAME-HUNGRY KILLER-COP RUNS BERSERK!
NOIR'S DIRTY COPS
TOM KING
ALSO IN THIS ISSUE
SPECIAL COMIX ISSUE
NOIR CITY
CRIMINAL
The FADE OUT
ED BRUBAKER
SEAN PHILLIPS
INTERVIEW
Noir City
NOTHING KIND ABOUT MAN
DANCING IN THE DARK
SCORING EVIL
SINNER'S LAMENT
SPECIAL MUSIC ISSUE
NOIR CITY
INTERNATIONAL NOIR
8 MILLION WAYS TO DIE
STERANKO'S 5 FAVORITE NOIRS
HOT SHADOWS
A PUBLICATION OF THE FILM NOIR FOUNDATION
NOIR CITY
NOIR CITY
CARNIVAL NOIR
NOIR CITY
WOMEN IN FILM NOIR
MURDER, SHE MADE
NOIR CITY
ALL STORIES COMPLETE!
THE DANCE OF DEATH
HARD LUCK DOGS
THE LAST OF SHEILA
UNDER COVERS OF DARKNESS

LIFE AFTER DEATH

By Dan Akira

What if you knew you'd been murdered while you were still alive? This is a premise that—unlike the protagonists of its many iterations—just won't die.

In *D.O.A.* (1949), Los Angeles accountant Frank Bigelow (Edmond O'Brien) flies to San Francisco on a working holiday. At a hotel bar, he's slipped a lethal mickey and spends the rest of the film racing against time to find his killer. Nearly two decades before *D.O.A.*, there was *Der Mann, der seinen Mörder sucht* (*The Man in Search of His Murderer*, 1931), directed by Robert Siodmak. The film was loosely based on the Jules Verne novel *Les Tribulations d'un Chinois en Chine* (1879), and sees a man attempt to rescind a hit that he put out on himself. These two films show how a basic premise could be revived, with details tailored to the setting and time period of each film. Same but different. It's this malleable framework that led director Kurt St. Thomas to remake *D.O.A.* in 2022, and compelled us at NOIR CITY to put it in the context of its varied predecessors.

Frank Bigelow is a role that, from his name alone, makes perfect sense for John Doe, a punk rock icon, author, and actor. He headlines St. Thomas's *D.O.A.*, a black-and-white reimagining of the 1949 original. Although set during the same postwar era, the location is changed from California to St. Augustine, Florida, where the director lives. Bigelow is once again tasked with finding the man who poisoned him, but this time around, he's a professional gumshoe. During a screening at the American Cinematheque in Hollywood in June 2023, the film's creators—St. Thomas, Doe, screenwriter Nicholas Griffin, actress Lucinda Jenney, and composer Jaimee Jimin Park—discussed the challenges of reviving such a beloved release. "I tried to write the screenplay three times," said St. Thomas, "and it was painfully awful. Then Nick came in and saved the day."

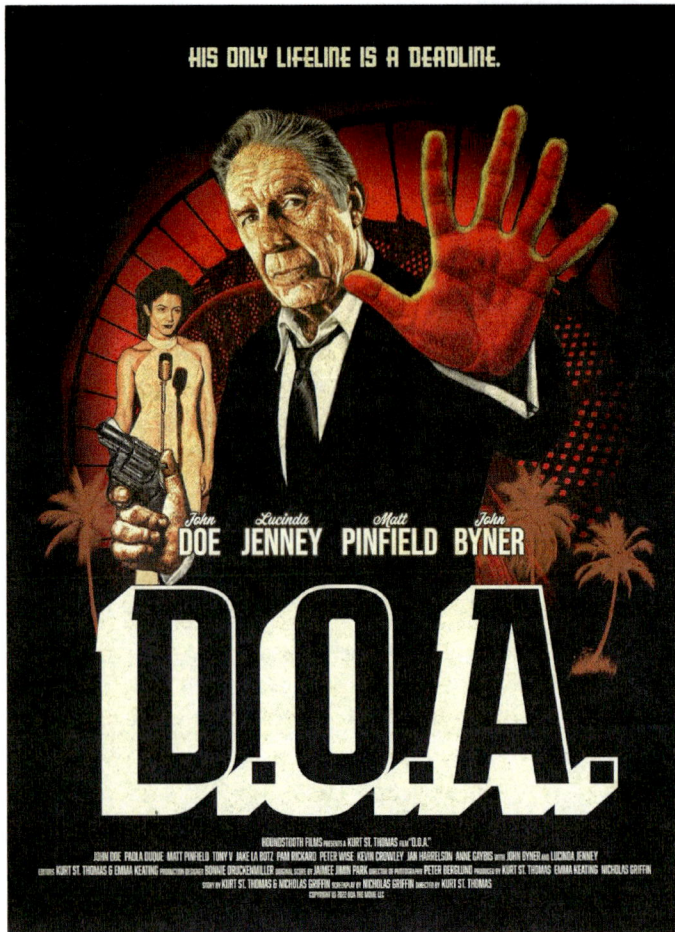

HIS ONLY LIFELINE IS A DEADLINE.

JOHN   Lucinda   Matt   John
DOE JENNEY PINFIELD BYNER

D.O.A.

HOUNDSTOOTH FILMS PRESENTS A KURT ST. THOMAS FILM "D.O.A."
JOHN DOE PAOLA DUQUE MATT PINFIELD TONY V JAKE LA BOTZ PAM RICKARD PETER WISE KEVIN CROWLEY IAN HARRELSON ANNE GRYBUS WITH JOHN BYNER AND LUCINDA JENNEY
EDITORS KURT ST. THOMAS & EMMA KEATING PRODUCTION DESIGNER BONNIE DRUCKEMILLER ORIGINAL SCORE BY JAIMEZ JIMIN PARK DIRECTOR OF PHOTOGRAPHY PETER BERGLUND PRODUCED BY KURT ST. THOMAS EMMA KEATING NICHOLAS GRIFFIN
STORY BY KURT ST. THOMAS & NICHOLAS GRIFFIN SCREENPLAY BY NICHOLAS GRIFFIN DIRECTED BY KURT ST. THOMAS
COPYRIGHT © 2022 DOA THE MOVIE LLC

"Kurt wanted it to be like *Chinatown*," Griffin recounted. "And I thought, oh God, is that all? And he needed it in three weeks." The screenwriter found it particularly difficult to determine the motive for the new Bigelow's murder. "[In] the original *D.O.A.*, [Bigelow] is poisoned for a very obscure reason," he noted. "And [now that he's] a detective on a case, that means you've got to have a mystery, you've got to have a client. And then you've got to have a reason for the guy being poisoned after he's been hired."

The breakthrough that Griffin needed was the casting of John Doe. The screenwriter was friends with the X frontman, and understood how to cater to Doe's strengths as an actor. The rest of the script fell into place from there. "I wasn't trying to hear Robert Mitchum in my head," he asserted. "I was just trying to hear John." Doe, now in his seventies, admitted (to much laughter) that he hadn't been offered leading man parts since turning forty. "That's the point [at which] you're relegated to doctors and dads," he noted. Weathered but still youthful, Doe has the physicality to play an old-school detective. Furthermore, some of X's best-known songs, like "Johnny Hit and Run Pauline" and "Los Angeles" showcased Doe's familiarity with punchy, pulp storytelling.

Chain-smoking behind the wheel of his boat-sized DeSoto, the doomed Bigelow narrates the film with philosophical mutterings like "You know what they say about the future. If you look far enough ahead, you might not be in it." There's obvious influence taken from Raymond Chandler novels, in both the voice-over and the dense plotting. The noir archetypes are present as well, from the frazzled female client and sadistic henchman to the tone-deaf chanteuse who can't carry a tune. St. Thomas even tips his cap to

the Chandler-inspired *The Big Lebowski* (1998) by subjecting his detective to interrogation via toilet bowl. A few crucial pieces carry over from the original *D.O.A.*, however, including the opening confession at the police station and the iridium poisoning at a bar full of annoying conventioneers. The swampy Florida setting, replete with alligators and quick-tempered locals, helps to give this *D.O.A.* an overriding sense of discomfort.

The supporting cast boasts familiar yet unconventional faces. Former MTV VJ Matt Pinfield, with his trademark shaved head and gravelly voice, plays Captain Parker, an irate cop who just wants to get home to his wife's pot roast. Comedian-impressionist John Byner, a frequent guest on the old *Tonight Show*, is resurrected in a bit of inspired casting as Arthur Majak, the smarmy gang boss who sums up Frank's predicament: "You've got one day left to live, which may make you the most dangerous man alive. Nothing to gain, nothing to lose." Neither Pinfield nor Byner possess stellar acting chops, but their distinct energies lend to the film's off-kilter rhythm.

Bigelow's predicament is afforded more sympathy during his scenes with the mysterious Grace (Jenney). The detective encounters her twice, and in both instances she manages to put him at ease. The die has already been cast with regard to Bigelow's fate, but in sharing a drink with the intuitive stranger, he's reminded of the little things he once took for granted. It's during these scenes that *D.O.A.* manages to carve out an identity independent of its 1949 predecessor. St. Thomas and Doe expend most of their energy on lightweight (albeit charming) pastiche, but Jenney's performance provides an emotional anchor that the film otherwise lacks. Bigelow and Grace agree to meet a third time, and the detective—seizing the opportunity for spiritual gains—desperately clings to survival in

Screenwriter Nicholas Griffin tailored the new version of Bigelow, a private detective, to suit the personality of his longtime friend Doe.

The iconic ending of the 1949 film, in which Bigelow (Edmond O'Brien) dies at a police station, has been tweaked slightly in each subsequent version.

order to keep their church rendezvous. His subsequent visit to the police station is inconsequential by comparison. "Never been happier," Bigelow mumbles, before slipping into the great beyond. The film knows it can't rival the punch of the original ending, so it takes a more wistful approach. It proves effective.

St. Thomas is not alone in his admiration for *D.O.A.*, which fell into the public domain due to a copyright snafu. Eddie Davis rehashed the film in Australia as *Color Me Dead* (1969), but it wasn't until Annabel Jankel and Rocky Morton came along that *D.O.A.* would be given a full Hollywood makeover. The directing duo adored Maté's film, and struck up a deal with Touchstone Pictures to reimagine it in the erotic thriller mold that dominated the box office during the 1980s.

It's a good thing, too, because the prologue, shot in black and white and framed in extreme close-up, plays like a parody of the original. Dexter Cornell (Dennis Quaid) stumbles to a police station to report his own death. Although the station is using contemporary video technology, Detective Ulmer (Brion James) and the other officers look as though they stepped out of an early TCM commercial. The attempt to recreate Maté's heightened formalism is admirable, but Jankel and Morton's interpretation is too exaggerated to succeed on its own.

After a clever transition to color, *D.O.A.* (1988) becomes a more conventional thriller. Cornell is a college professor living in Austin, Texas. Quaid, coming off his red-hot turn as a N'awlins cop in *The Big Easy* (1987), is only slightly less effective as an academic

> "Jankel and Morton may be playing within a subgenre predicated on glamour, but the best moments in *D.O.A.* stem from the same low-budget ingenuity as the original.

who elicits flirtatious giggles from his students. Sydney Fuller (Meg Ryan) is one of these students, though she takes on the roles of kidnap victim, assistant, and love interest as the film progresses. Charlotte Rampling delivers arguably the finest performance in the film as Mrs. Fitzwaring, the socialite mother of a student who died on Cornell's watch. Rampling is not only chilling in her scenes, but her character brings about the narrative twists that distinguish this version from the others.

The characterization of Cornell is where the film's time period proves most impactful. He's not Bigelow, a blue-collar everyman who dreams of something more, but a self-absorbed success who exudes confidence to the point of cockiness. He's a yuppie academic, privileged enough to elicit jealousy in public while he struggles to write another book in private. He should be unlikable, but the 1980s were typified by male protagonists who drew sympathy from their audience despite their inflated egos. Erotic thrillers in particular were predicated on seeing bad things happen to people who were well-off.

It may seem contrived that a peer of Cornell's would resort to murder to advance their writing career, but considering both academics are in the throes of the "greed decade," the third act revelation makes contextual sense. Still, Cornell is unable to hide his amusement. "Just somebody's homework, that was all," he ruminates, before exiting the police station. He doesn't even get to collapse in front of the puzzled officers who took down his story, making his eventual demise all

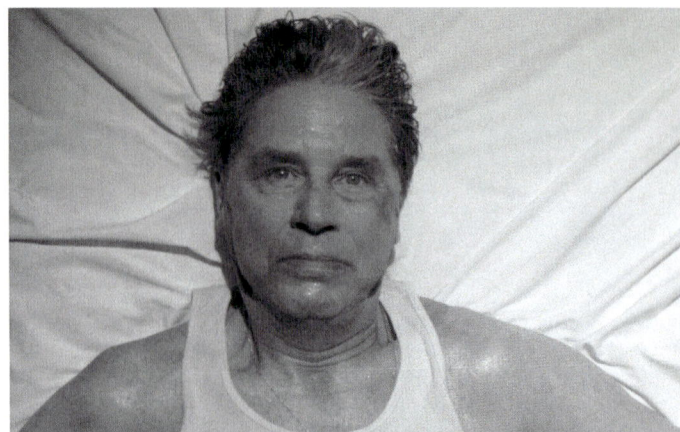

Kurt St. Thomas's wistful remake of *D.O.A.* proves that there's still plenty of dramatic potential within the original premise.

the more pointless.

Jankel and Morton may be playing within a subgenre predicated on glamour, but the best moments in *D.O.A.* stem from the same low-budget ingenuity as the original. There are "stolen shots"—or shots obtained without proper permits—littered throughout the film, just as there were in the 1949 version. The directors were forced to use long lenses to ensure that they could capture their frantic protagonist on the streets of Austin, which gives their chase scenes a sense of unpredictability. They also took advantage of the local music scene, setting a moody exchange between Cornell and Mrs. Fitzwaring's daughter during a concert by the indie duo Timbuk 3. It's these tactile flourishes, rather than the strained re-creations of its opener, that make the film an entertaining if inferior remake.

The legacy of *D.O.A.* transcends medium and genre. The 1949 film spawned the play *DOA: A Noir Musical*, which received two ATAC Globe Awards in 2012, as well as the cult franchise *Crank* (2006), which took the premise and applied it to a series of self-aware action-comedies. There was even a 1951 episode of the radio show *The Adventures of Sam Spade* in which the titular shamus is visited by a man who has already been murdered. The 1988 and 2022 versions differ from the rest, however, because they attempt to play within the same film noir confines as the original.

Neither manage to top Mate's chaotic masterpiece. Few films have. They do, however, showcase the endless possibilities of *D.O.A.* as a premise. St. Thomas took a "wrong man, wrong place" storyline and applied it to an aging private detective. The result is a tender tribute piece littered with cult figures from the 1970s and 1980s. Jankel and Morton, meanwhile, revved up their version with white-collar crime, action set pieces, and a steamy central romance. They wound up with a mainstream crowd-pleaser that boosted the careers (and spurred the marriage) of stars Quaid and Ryan. Enjoyment of these films ultimately hinges on the willingness to get on their specific wavelengths.

In his book *Hollywood and the Movies of the Fifties* (2023), Foster Hirsch attributes the appeal of *D.O.A.* to its existential dread. "Positing a world in which Bigelow's 'crime' receives disproportionate punishment," he writes. "*D.O.A.* is pitch-black film noir." No matter the circumstances or setting, the notion of hunting one's own killer is so cosmically cruel that it'll forever prompt self-reflection within the viewer. It's the reason filmmakers keep returning to the scene of the crime and reviving this cinematic corpse for another spin around the block. At this rate, the corpse will outlive us all. ∎

DENNIS QUAID   MEG RYAN

Someone poisoned Dexter Cornell.
He's got to find out who.
He's got to find out why.
He's got to find out now.
In 24 hours, he'll be
Dead On Arrival.

D.O.A.

TOUCHSTONE PICTURES presents
In association with SILVER SCREEN PARTNERS III a Z'DUN/SCANLED Production
DENNIS QUAID · MEG RYAN "D.O.A." DANIEL STERN and CHARLOTTE RAMPLING
Story by CHARLES EDWARD POGUE and RUSSELL ROUSE & CLARENCE GREENE Screenplay by CHARLES EDWARD POGUE Produced by IAN SANDER & LAURA ZISKIN
Directed by ROCKY MORTON · ANNABEL JANKEL DOLBY STEREO TOUCHSTONE PICTURES
R RESTRICTED

RINGSIDE SEAT magazine presents **RINGSIDE CINEMA**, the first book dedicated to boxing movie posters and lobby cards from the past 100 years. Rarely seen international posters are also represented here. This beautiful, 170-page book includes an introduction by TCM host and author Eddie Muller and foreword by Steve Kronenberg, *Noir City* magazine's managing editor and frequent contributor to RINGSIDE SEAT magazine. From Alfred Hitchcock's *The Ring* to film noir's *The Set-Up* to 2010's *Creed*, it's all here and a feast for the eyes. RINGSIDE CINEMA is essential for every boxing fan and movie aficionado's bookshelf.

"Kudos to *Ringside Seat* and designer Michael Kronenberg for creating a book that combines three of my great passions: boxing, movies, and poster art. This one's a keeper."

–Eddie Muller

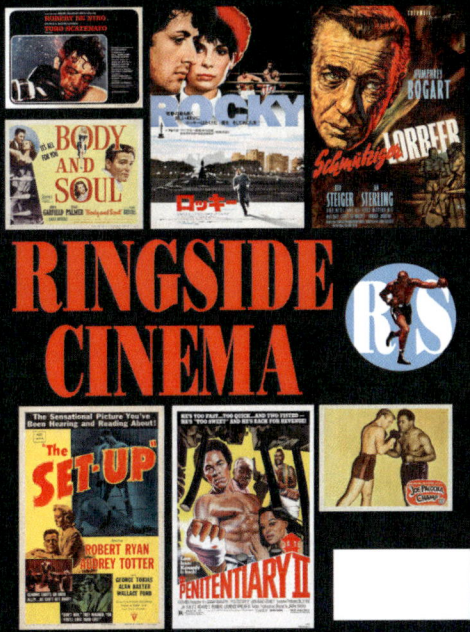

Order RINGSIDE CINEMA on AMAZON

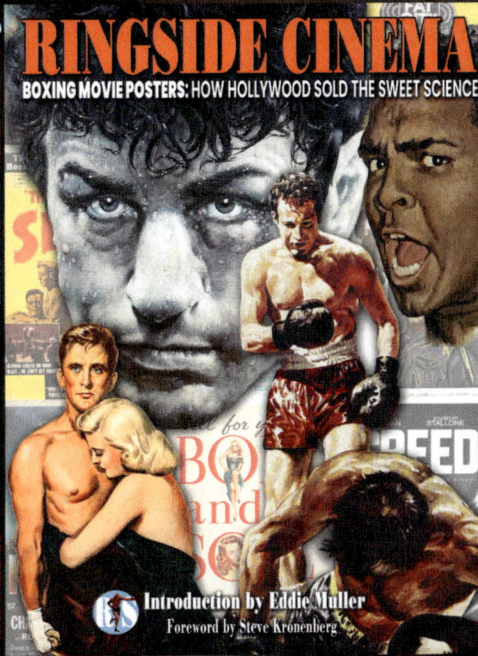

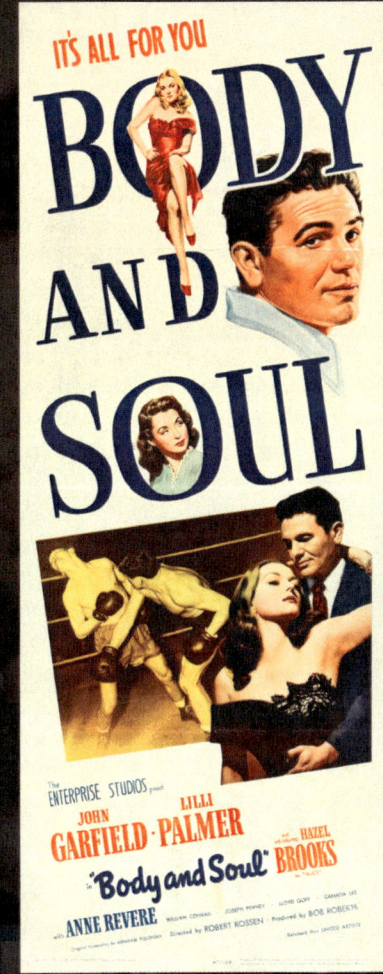

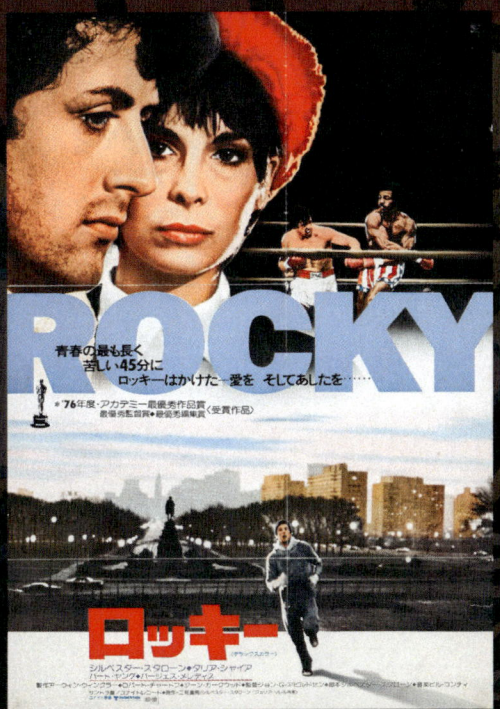

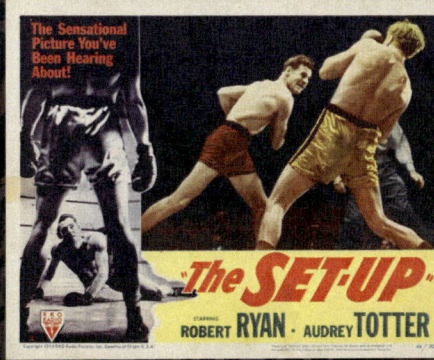

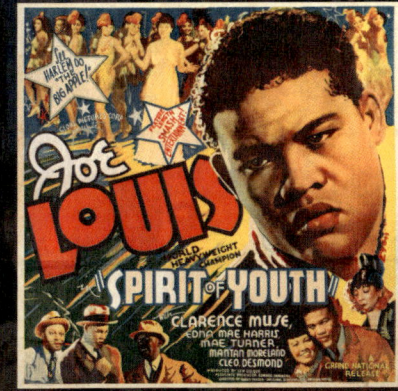

BREAKING

By Drew A. Smith

"I want out. I want a new life," says Violet (Jennifer Tilly) in the Wachowskis' lesbian neo-noir film *Bound* (1996). As far as crime thrillers go, this one ticks all the noir boxes: passionate love, all-consuming lust, murder. A mob wife and supreme opportunist, Violet is a true femme fatale—her wit and sexuality have served her well, but now all she seeks is freedom. Enter Corky (Gina Gershon), an ex-con and certifiable butch who is conspicuously good with her hands. She plans to whisk Violet out of the proverbial closet with the promise of everlasting female companionship and, of course, the blood-soaked $2 million that Violet's gangster husband has recently secured through nefarious means. Needless to say, their scheme goes awry and the two embark on a thrilling (and steamy) gay crime fest for the ages.

Same-sex desire is nothing new to noir—before Violet and Corky there was Susan Sarandon and Geena Davis in *Thelma & Louise* (1991), and before them, Lauren Bacall as a bisexual socialite in *Young Man with a Horn* (1950) and Judith Anderson as the voyeuristic Mrs. Danvers in Alfred Hitchcock's *Rebecca* (1940). What *Bound* brought to the screen were actual truck-driving, leather-donning, out-and-proud lesbians, not the (not-so) subliminally queer-coded characters of the past. But as revolutionary as they may be, Violet and Corky don't exactly break any molds; Corky is still the classically macho noir hero whose susceptibility to Violet's feminine allure pulls her deeper into a world of grave danger. And it isn't until the end of the film that we see how Violet might dress and act without the stereotypical limitations of her role. Like a decorative figurine, the femme fatale has often been relegated to her sexually expressive—albeit predictable—purpose within the narrative. This is not to insinuate that the femme fatale's body is the sole locus of her power; her cunning intelligence and agency are just as vital to her persona as her cleavage. But the impositions placed upon her as an object of the male gaze have rightfully left her (and audiences) wanting more. One thing is for certain: the femme fatale has wanted *out* of her box for a very long time. It's as if filmmakers have purposefully been toying with her; they have been tampering with her characterization and adorning her with queerness as a means of uncovering her authenticity for decades. But the teasing and torment may have finally come to an end with the release of the new film *Love Lies Bleeding* (2024), in which the femme fatale finally busts loose in her newest form.

Rose Glass has quickly proven herself to be one of the most provocative new filmmakers, made clear in her debut *Saint Maud* (2019). Though not a noir, it features similar themes of lesbianism, lies, and murder, demonstrating Glass's acute appreciation for the queerness inherent in a world of suspicion and anarchy. Though only her second directorial feature, *Love Lies Bleeding* pushes the envelope even further. The film takes place somewhere in the outskirts of Albuquerque in 1989, and stars real-life queer Kristen Stewart as another Louise, Lou for short. Lou is more outwardly androgynous than her predecessor; instead of a diner waitress she's a low-key tomboy and high-key stud working as a gym manager and occasional steroid dealer. Newcomer Katy O'Brian (also a real-life queer) plays opposite as Jackie, a body-building runaway with aspirational dreams and a bad temper with whom Lou becomes

In *Bound*, Gina Gershon and Jennifer Tilly portrayed explicitly queer variations on the classic macho noir hero and the femme fatale . . .

. . . while the love between *Thelma & Louise* (Susan Sarandon and Geena Davis), made five years earlier, remained implicit.

FREE

Jackie (Katy O'Brian) and
Lou (Kristen Stewart) are
lovers in deep trouble in
Love Lies Bleeding.

As Lou Sr., Ed Harris adds another scary villain to his ever-lengthening résumé of noir characters.

infatuated. Their affair blossoms quickly under the distinctly 1980s glow of fluorescent gym lights no doubt riddled with fly carcasses. But through the film's sweat and grime emerges its noir heart—you see, Lou's estranged father isn't a very nice man; he's an illegal arms dealer with a knack for making people disappear. Oh, and Jackie works for him as a waitress at the local shooting range he owns. Throw in some flashback sequences and existential philosophy and we have the basic structure of a classic noir: a cynical hero; a crime boss with whom (s)he is inextricably tied; a shared, dreadful secret; and a femme fatale in a position just vulnerable enough to make anyone do something stupid for her.

When considered as a series, *Thelma & Louise*, *Bound*, and *Love Lies Bleeding* create a progressive model for queer film noir that both upholds and subverts the form's essential tropes. In their own ways, Thelma (Davis) and Louise (Sarandon) are both femme fatales, though the slightly older, more controlling Louise whose actions kickstart the narrative certainly fills the void left by the absence of a male hero. On the other hand, Thelma—the more naturally femme of the two—grows significantly over the course of the film, learning to use her charm and good looks to commit armed robbery. And though it is Louise's idea to embark on their dangerous affair, it is Thelma who ultimately leads them over the edge. But as clear as it may be that the pair is meant to be together forever, back in 1991 a final (platonic?) kiss was the most explicit queer love we were going to see between hero and femme fatale.

Released five years after *Thelma & Louise*, *Bound* does not constrain its sapphic nature—Violet is hot as hell and Corky cannot

deny her the feminine touch she craves. Though the film's unapologetic homoeroticism might free Violet from the inadequate caresses of a man, it does not allow her to escape the confines of male desire. As a fetish object, she fulfills all the classical expectations: she wears skin-tight dresses or lingerie, always has a drink in hand for her man, and with her every step the pleasurable clacking of a stiletto heel upon marble floors suggests both power and mystery. But in this cleverly self-aware film, Violet's styling is coded as performance—

> When considered as a series, *Thelma & Louise*, *Bound*, and *Love Lies Bleeding* create a progressive model for queer film noir that both upholds and subverts the form's essential tropes.

a means of survival—rather than her true nature. Through her concealment she embodies the underlying desire of every femme fatale before her—not just for the typical luxuries of money, good sex, and sadistic power, but above all else to be *unbound*. If *Bound* showed us the femme fatale's struggle for freedom, *Love Lies Bleeding* shows us what she might do once she's got it. In other words: as the penultimate model for the lesbian femme fatale, Violet walked so that Jackie could run.

Aside from dabbling in same-sex attraction, Jackie is a truly *queer* femme fatale. She is hardly the traditional image of femininity; her bulging muscles and lack of interest in men brazenly refute this classification. Notoriously a receptacle for fetishism and control, the queer body on its own cannot escape the gaze—*Bound* illustrates this. But in *Love Lies Bleeding*, Jackie's virile body is made doubly repulsive to the typical male viewer; it is outside their control and, we will soon learn, her own. Despite this, Jackie demonstrates textbook traits of the femme fatale: she is manipulative as a means to get what she wants, uses emotionless sex as payment, and gets herself into precarious situations of escalating severity. So it goes; trouble is always going to find the femme fatale—but then again, so will the hero. Her vulnerability is what draws Lou in—who doesn't want to feel like they can save someone? Traditional male chivalry has been part of the relationship between the heroic chump and his femme fatale

In *Bound*, Gershon is Corky, a character that fifty years earlier might have been played by John Garfield.

since the classic noir era and has continued into modernity. Even with queer couples this dynamic is repeated; Louise is the one to save Thelma and Corky does the same for Violet. But in contemporary queer neo-noir, *saving* doesn't exactly imply any form of courtesy. Rather, *releasing* might be the better word, as Lou's way of doing so involves pushing Jackie's body beyond its capacities, both physical and sexual, by injecting her with steroids and later declaring "I want to stretch you."

As in *Thelma & Louise*, the crime spree at the center of *Love Lies Bleeding* begins with the killing of an abusive male. But not with a gun this time—as Jackie puts it, "anyone can feel strong hiding behind a piece of metal." Unlike the quiet and more mysterious femme fatales of the past, Jackie is not afraid to get her hands really, really dirty. The jaw-dropping violence she commits in seemingly uncontrollable, drug-induced fits of rage attests to the pent-up frustrations of the femme fatale following decades of servitude to men. Glass's use of body horror grotesquely resists any further submission—we can actually see Jackie's veins and tendons twisting and crawling beneath the confines of her skin, morphing her into something bigger and more powerful than she has ever been before.

Compelled to save her new girlfriend from execution, Lou seizes the opportunity to frame her father for the murder, in the process taking down the family's crime empire. Both as individuals and as a

Stewart fulfills the role of the traditional male hero in *Love Lies Bleeding*, commiting a crime to "save" the femme fatale.

By the end of *Love Lies Bleeding*, cinema's history of minimizing women is quite literally reversed; with Lou at her side, Jackie is maximally transformed into the ultimate femme fatale.

pair, Lou and Jackie blur the boundaries between woman and man, femme fatale and hero. Queer characters can never be stock characters! Therefore, we must reject any expectations that they'll behave according to any prescriptions. Just as Jackie complicates the usual idea of the femme fatale with her tendency toward feral violence, Lou is not an average hero. For example, she also begins using sex and manipulation as a means to cover up Jackie's crimes, an MO typically reserved for the femme fatale, not the hero. As both characters adopt habits typical of their counterpart, we begin to see the freedom of queer noir: the ability for a single person to embody both sides of a dichotomy. And rather than dilute the function of either, doing so actually enhances their potency. Serving as both each other's problem and solution, and in a universe governed by vices, Lou and Jackie have distilled in them the essence of noir. But although their attraction to each other might seem ill-fated and their relationship doomed by noir standards, their *need* to be together is more powerful than any generic label or limitation. If classic noir harnessed that need as an ultimately destructive (and self-destructive) tension between a man and a woman, queer noir fulfills it by finally allowing the hero and femme fatale to be together. As a queer couple who both enhance and transcend classic noir, the longing that underscores every pairing before them is made irrevocable and the true purpose of the femme fatale is revealed: she is the hero's hero and the

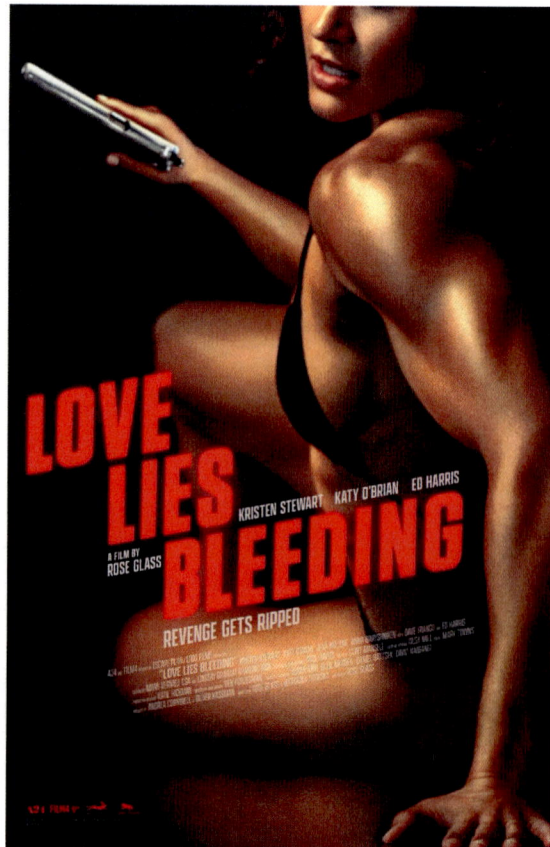

only way out of this world of cyclical misery.

By the end of *Love Lies Bleeding*, cinema's history of minimizing women is quite literally reversed; with Lou at her side, Jackie is maximally transformed into the ultimate femme fatale. But not *fatale* in the sense of connoting certain death; rather, *fatale* as an end to the ceaseless relegation of women, particularly sexually liberated and queer women, to inferior positions of power and as servants to the male gaze. If classic noir made it clear that feminine sexuality can be a tool, queer noir shows us new ways to wield it. Thus, Jackie and Lou represent a new beginning for noir couples. Their queerness renders their sexuality not so much a tool for their treachery against evil men, but a reason for it. Like the trailblazing films that came before it, *Love Lies Bleeding* continues the trend of women-led noirs that break down long-standing tropes in new and invigorating ways. With unabashedly queer characters, Rose Glass has redefined classic aesthetics and created new possibilities for noir women in the process. Through her queered vision we can appreciate these ferocious women as something more than they have ever been permitted to be: post-human, post-hero, and most importantly, post–femme fatale. Nevermore shall the femme fatale be trapped within a closet of someone else's design—it was always too small for her anyway. And how interesting it will be to see where she goes next, now that she's finally broken free. ■

MARSHLAND

Marshland, or *La isla mínima* (2014), has all the trappings of a traditional film noir. A central mystery. A pair of detectives, one prone to cutting corners and the other committed to the legal process. A Mr. Big who presides over townsfolk with an iron fist, and a slowly unraveling conspiracy involving drugs, sex, and money. What sets the film apart from its US predecessors, however, is the setting and political backdrop. *Marshland* takes place in 1980 Spain, shortly after the dictatorship of Francisco Franco dissolved. It intertwines the aforementioned investigation with the country's arduous transition to democracy, and the result is a fascinating snapshot of an era in which the country's moral compass was being recalibrated.

The film's English-language title is explained quickly. The viewer is immediately presented with an aerial view of lush, green landscapes. Waterways twist and turn like the nervous system of a single, living organism. Seen from above, this is an arresting terrain, but the images were not obtained from a drone or helicopter. Instead, director Alberto Rodríguez and cinematographer Alex Catalán took the illustrations of Argentine artist Héctor Garrido and stitched them together to showcase the serenity of the Guadalquivir Marshes from afar. The frame inches closer to the region as the credits roll, however, and by the time we land on the ground, abstract beauty has devolved into burnt grass and decayed machinery. Before a single line is uttered, the romanticism of Spain has been overtaken by the grimness of reality.

The setting of *Marshland* evokes the first season of *True Detective* (2014–)—

SECCIÓN OFICIAL

62 DONOSTIA ZINEMALDIA
FESTIVAL DE SAN SEBASTIAN
INTERNATIONAL FILM FESTIVAL

UN THRILLER DE ALBERTO RODRÍGUEZ

LA ISLA MÍNIMA

NADIE HABLA...
TODOS OCULTAN ALGO

Pedro Suárez (Raúl Arévalo, left) represents the young, democratic Spain, while Juan Robles (Javier Gutiérrez) is a remnant of the country's Francoist past.

geographically remote and culturally isolated—but the decay is not limited to the scenery. The denizens of the Guadalquivir Marshes, commonly referred to as Spain's "Deep South," are impoverished and disillusioned. They've borne the brunt of the country's upheaval since Franco's death five years earlier, and politics continue to take precedence over their personal struggles. The decision to set the film's inciting incident on September 20, 1980, the same day as the real-life Markina attack, is no coincidence. By contrasting local police work with the politically motivated murder of civil guards, *Marshland* emphasizes the ideological split between Spain's two law enforcement agencies. This in turn mirrors the larger split within the country. Juan Robles (Javier Gutiérrez) warns his younger partner, Pedro Suárez (Raúl Arévalo), not to run afoul of the military during their investigation. Though initially posed as helpful, the former's comment proves to be the first of many that call his own fealty into question.

Robles and Suárez are homicide detectives sent from Madrid to locate two missing sisters. Robles represents the Francoite ideal of conservatism, patriotism, and traditional masculinity. He berates suspects and comfortably resorts to violence when pressed for results. Even his physiognomy—shorter, more squat and rugged—speaks to an earlier era, before diets became more varied and the middle class emerged. He is the "bad cop." Suárez, meanwhile, is the "good cop." He values progress and justice. He's tall, fair-haired, and constantly checking in with his family via telephone. He's also, crucially, out of step with the locals. The detectives' hotel room is adorned with a crucifix, surrounded by photos of Franco, Benito Mussolini, Adolf Hitler, and Portuguese dictator António de Oliveira Salazar. "Your new country," Suárez disapprovingly mumbles. Upon paying a visit to the sisters' classroom, the detective clocks two photos above the teacher's desk. Franco, to the right, and the country's new leader, Juan Carlos I, to the left. Who, in these marshes, deserves the public's allegiance?

Rodríguez and cowriter Rafael Cobos depict post-Francoist tensions the same way that classic noir utilized postwar trauma, which is to say, cynically. The detectives encounter those who are politically passionate, but most of the marshes' inhabitants are indifferent because their lives haven't improved. The fishing boats run on the same schedule, criminal exploitation is still rampant. The disappearance of two teens is tragic, sure, but not tragic enough to interrupt the side hustles that mediums and poacher-hunters have set up. The sisters' parents initially appear inconvenienced by the presence of Robles and Suárez, and it's only through repeated visits that the detectives are able to coerce details from their mother. The resistance from the sisters' father, on the other hand, only reaffirms the disposability of human life in the marshes. Especially when measured against material gain.

These fraught exchanges play out in broad daylight. *Marshland* is a hot, sticky film, and consequently, the detectives trying to play it cool can't make it through a scene without perspiring. It's a minor detail, but one that repeatedly serves to remind the viewer of their outsider status. Rodríguez's decision to eschew a more stylized approach stems from his fascination with the *Después de . . .* (1979–80) documentaries by Cecilia and José Juan Bartolomé. The series chronicled Spanish history during the same period in which *Marshland* is set, and served as a reference point for both the look and feel of the characters. This not only grounds the film in reality, but also makes the fleeting moments of visual

Suárez and Robles give chase in the climax. Director Alberto Rodríguez based several of the film's crucial frames on the work of photographer Atín Aya.

flair all the more memorable. Robles being entranced by a flamboyance of flamingos, for example, stands out because the beautifully lit encounter at dusk immediately cuts to a dingy police station. There's also a pulse-pounding chase set amid a tangle of reeds. The disorientation of the characters, and the firefight that ensues, evokes the climax of Joseph H. Lewis's classic *Gun Crazy* (1950), also set in a marsh.

The procedural elements of *Marshland* are well executed, if predictable. The film hits standard noir beats, whether it be the detectives bumping heads, the father becoming increasingly consumed by guilt, or the introduction of a rotund crime boss who dresses like a Sydney Greenstreet character. The application of these beats, however, is enlivened by the historical backdrop Rodríguez evokes. The decision to explore Robles's past, in particular, gives the film its most compelling dramatic conflict. The detective spearheads the film's final act and is even given a climactic showdown with the kidnapper of the two sisters. He triumphs, and is promptly celebrated by his peers. Most films would consider it subversive enough to have an unheroic character perform a heroic act, but *Marshland* digs deeper. Suárez discovers that his partner was formerly a member of Spain's notori-

ous Political-Social Brigade, which was a police force dedicated to persecuting and stifling anti-fascist opposition.

The film's penultimate scene, a celebratory night out, reckons with these coexisting truths. Robles dances and drinks in the distance, while Suárez sits at a barstool and sifts through photos of his partner executing his fellow countrymen. Devastated, Suárez seeks from his colleagues some flicker of acknowledgment or regret. Instead, Robles is blissful. Drenched in neon red light, the detective flirts with a female patron while puffing on a cigarette. *Marshland* transcends its genre limitations in this moment. By refusing a more conventional ending, and absolving Robles of punishment, the film forces the viewer to consider the ways in which "right" and "wrong" shift depending on who's in power.

Robles used the same tactics he learned as part of the Political-Social Brigade to solve the case of the missing sisters. He kills in both instances, but as far as he's concerned, both serve the greater good. Robles is an invaluable piece of Spain's past *and* present; a man willing to rewrite his personal code for results. *Marshland* was written by two men who grew up during La Movida, the cultural shift that helped to forge the country's post-Francoist identity,

and the final scene captures the complicated perspective through which they view their ancestors. The detectives stare at each other as they sidle up to their squad car. Finally, Robles breaks the silence. "We're good, right?" No response. Robles tosses off a knowing smirk before opening the door. He knows Suárez will keep quiet about his Brigade past, and he's right. The junior partner has become complicit in everything he previously stood against.

The detectives drive away, and *Marshland* returns to the aerial view from its opening credits. This time, however, what we see is not Garrido's illustrations but the real, imperfect landscape. The beauty the film previously advertised, and Suárez previously believed in, has been sullied by the truth. *Marshland* is not the first procedural to critique government institutions—nor will it be the last—but the specificity of its time and place, coupled with the film's unflinching examination of those who were "just following orders," is wholly unique. It's neo-noir filtered through the lens of historical drama, or historical drama filtered through the lens of neo-noir, depending on which aspect you gravitate toward. That the film can be enjoyed as both is a testament to its exemplary construction. ∎

NOIR OR NOT

Steve Kronenberg

THE HIDDEN

Marry science fiction and film noir and the nuptials will likely be held on the stygian side of Dark City. A recent example of this unholy union is Apple TV+'s series *Sugar* (2024–), which focuses on an intergalactic PI (Colin Farrell) who takes a deep dive into the dark heart of the human species. The show inverts the premise of Jack Sholder's *The Hidden* (1987), a police procedural cum alien invader film that continually fires on all cylinders while paying tribute to classic noir themes. The director's breakneck approach is evident from the get-go. As the opening credits unfold, we witness a bank robbery through the grainy lens of a security camera. Before grabbing a bag of cash, the grinning gunman casually murders a security guard and some innocent bystanders. But this is no professional perp: he's Jack DeVries (Chris Mulkey), ordinarily a law-abiding citizen, but one who's been invaded by an extraterrestrial parasite partial to pandemonium, heavy metal music, and stolen Ferraris. After driving at warp speed through Los Angeles and crashing a police blockade, DeVries is taken down by a hail of bullets from detective Tom Beck (Michael Nouri) and his colleagues in the LAPD. We soon learn that over a span of two weeks, DeVries has killed twenty-three people—including two children—and robbed eight banks. Beck and his boss (Clu Gulager) are baffled by how a man with no criminal record could suddenly turn LA upside down. Their puzzlement grows when they're joined by mysterious FBI agent Lloyd Gallagher (Kyle MacLachlan), who seems to know more than he's willing to reveal and may be harboring a secret. The creature they're trailing is a serial body thief, jumping into and out of a succession of unsuspecting human hosts.

The Hidden is highlighted by fine performances from its lead actors. Nouri and MacLachlan are a study in opposites, playing off each other. Beck is the hard-boiled, cynical cop who refuses to believe his quarry is an ET with an attitude. We feel his mounting frustration and

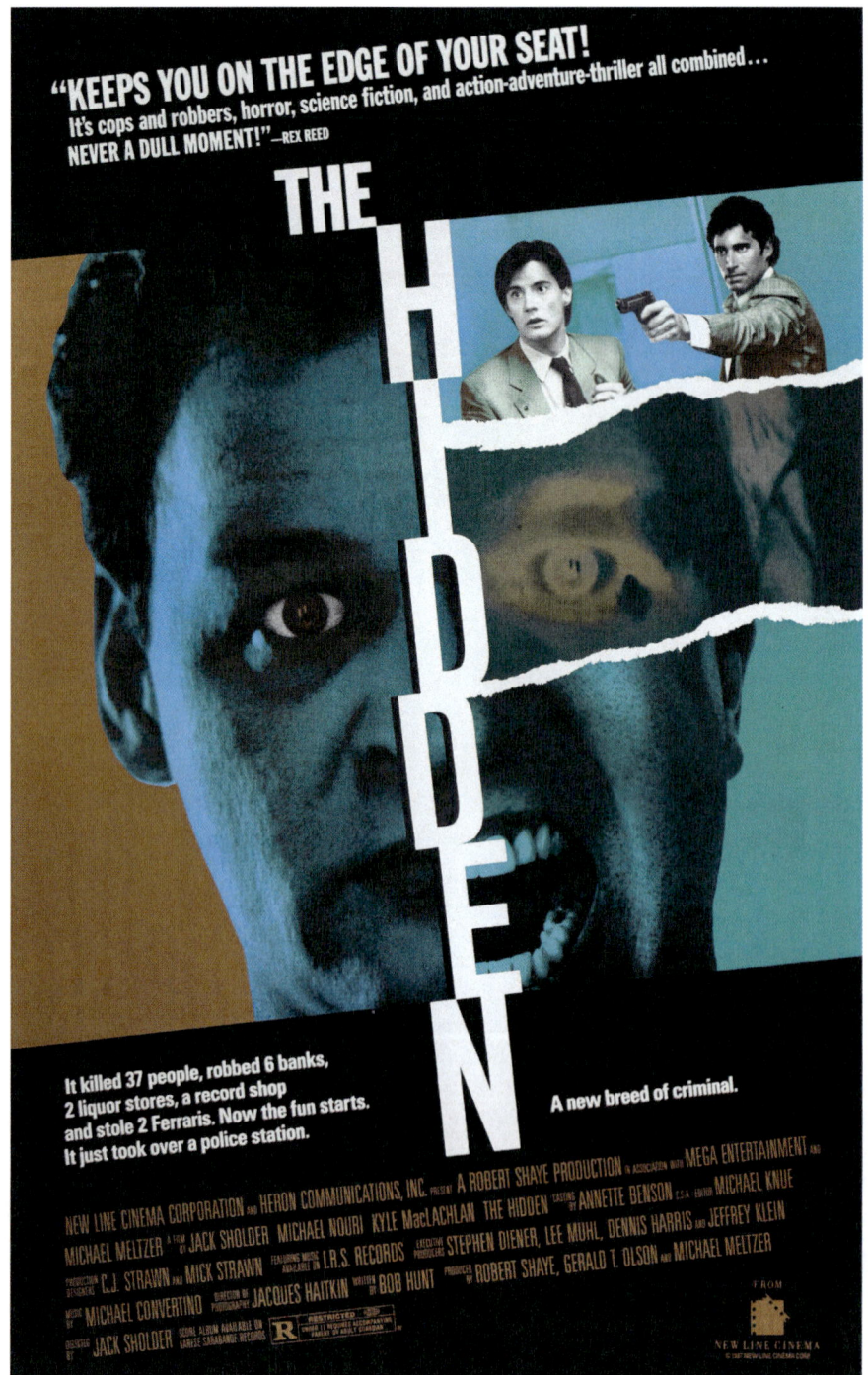

"KEEPS YOU ON THE EDGE OF YOUR SEAT! It's cops and robbers, horror, science fiction, and action-adventure-thriller all combined... NEVER A DULL MOMENT!" —REX REED

THE HIDDEN

It killed 37 people, robbed 6 banks, 2 liquor stores, a record shop and stole 2 Ferraris. Now the fun starts. It just took over a police station.

A new breed of criminal.

NEW LINE CINEMA CORPORATION and HERON COMMUNICATIONS, INC. PRESENT A ROBERT SHAYE PRODUCTION IN ASSOCIATION WITH MEGA ENTERTAINMENT AND MICHAEL MELTZER A FILM BY JACK SHOLDER MICHAEL NOURI KYLE MacLACHLAN THE HIDDEN CASTING BY ANNETTE BENSON EDITED BY MICHAEL KNUE PRODUCTION DESIGNERS C.J. STRAWN AND MICK STRAWN FEATURING MUSIC AVAILABLE ON I.R.S. RECORDS EXECUTIVE PRODUCERS STEPHEN DIENER, LEE MUHL, DENNIS HARRIS AND JEFFREY KLEIN MUSIC BY MICHAEL CONVERTINO DIRECTION OF PHOTOGRAPHY JACQUES HAITKIN WRITTEN BY BOB HUNT PRODUCED BY ROBERT SHAYE, GERALD T. OLSON AND MICHAEL MELTZER DIRECTED BY JACK SHOLDER SOUND ALBUM AVAILABLE ON VARESE SARABANDE RECORDS [R] RESTRICTED

NEW LINE CINEMA

Locked in and loaded: Armed cops Kyle MacLachlan and Michael Nouri are trapped in a local jail while pursuing a decidedly unfriendly E.T.

anger as he tries to deal with Gallagher's tight-lipped demeanor. MacLachlan offers a deft balance of naivete, childlike guilelessness, and stony determination. His face remains a blank canvas, his eyes focused and fixed, yet the unspoken, eye-to-eye bond he shares with Beck's young daughter (Kristen Clayton) provides some welcome poignance. MacLachlan's quirky and affecting performance as Jeffrey Beaumont in David Lynch's *Blue Velvet* (1986) may have provided a template for the character of Gallagher. But Gallagher is a stronger character than Beaumont, as well as a prelude to MacLachlan's equally bizarre work as Special Agent Dale Cooper in Lynch's *Twin Peaks* (1990–91). Sholder later said that MacLachlan played Gallagher as if he were living through tragedy, donning a mask to hide his true self. According to Nouri, he and MacLachlan mete while waiting to audition, "and we talked about it and we both liked it and we said to each other, 'I'll do it if you do it.' We made the pact, and they cast both of us and that's how that came about."

Unlike the aliens in *Invasion of the Body Snatchers* (1956), the creature in *The Hidden* doesn't turn its victims into soulless replicants. Each of the alien's hosts is given a distinctive persona by the film's solid supporting cast. William Boyett is accountant Jonathan Miller, described by his doctor as "kind and gentle." But after the invader enters his body, a wholly different side of Miller emerges.

Wearing a sadistic grin, he casually beats a record store clerk to death, shoots a Ferrari dealer before stealing one of his cars, and subjects everyone around him to the sights and sounds of his gastritis condition. Avoiding eye contact with Miller is the best way to remain alive and unharmed. B-movie bad girl Claudia Christian (*Maniac Cop 2*) delivers a provocative performance as exotic dancer Brenda Lee Van Buren. Once inside her, the alien is instantly intrigued by its new female body, and Christian captures the entity's curiosity by fondling her breasts with a look of surprise and delight. She later flays and fillets a would-be rapist before becoming an AR-wielding one-woman army, decimating as many cops and bystanders as her ammo supply will allow. Clarence Felder is Lieutenant John Masterson, who's introduced as affable and good-natured, eagerly engaged in camaraderie with his fellow officers. Once he's in the creature's clutches, he exudes the arrogance of a cop on a power trip. Armed with a variety of assault weapons, he stalks the corridors of the Lincoln Heights Jail, taking down both prisoners and police as he hunts for Gallagher and Beck. Masterson is also the only one of the alien's hosts who speaks with Gallagher. "We can take over this planet," he declares. "There's

As host to an alien parasite, an armed and extremely dangerous Claudia Christian takes down a host of victims in *The Hidden*.

MacLachlan is cornered by some serious firepower during the film's frenetic climax.

Impervious to bullets, possessed cop Ed O'Ross looks determined to decimate some fellow police officers.

nothing to stop us." Most disturbing of all is John McCann portraying a popular presidential candidate in whose body the creature intends to remain--all the way to the White House. "*I want to be President!*" he hollers to a cheering crowd at a press conference, licking his lips and donning a demonic smile. It's a genuinely unnerving moment, now more relevant than in the 1980s.

Jim Kouf, under the pseudonym Bob Hunt, is credited with the screenplay, but Sholder extensively reworked it. Both Kouf and New Line Cinema saw the film as a buddy cop–horror hybrid. Sholder envisioned it as a study in the frailty of identity and the tenuous hold we have on our own humanity—themes familiar to noiristas and previously explored in masterworks like *M* (1931), *Shadow of a Doubt* (1943), and *In a Lonely Place* (1950). By condensing

Kouf's treatment into a compact tale of two cops tracking a serial killer, Sholder also follows the template of such classic noirs as *The Naked City* (1948), *He Walked by Night* (1948), and *Follow Me Quietly* (1949). *The Hidden*'s alien predator possesses all the traits of the most ruthless noir antagonists: greed, hubris, cruelty, and an unquenchable thirst for power.

Jacques Haitkin's cinematography drops *The Hidden* squarely into the noir *policier* subgenre. The photography skillfully blends car chases at Mach 1 speed with slower, more subdued prowling through LA's seamiest side streets. Haitkin uses wide-angle shots to capture a shootout in MacArthur Park, a greasy strip club on Las Palomas Boulevard, a record store on Melrose Avenue, the police station in Lincoln Heights. Hand-held camerawork puts us in the middle of a

claustrophobic gunfight through the narrow corridors of the Lincoln Heights Jail, a nod to films as diverse as *Riot in Cell Bock 11* (1954) and *Assault on Precinct 13* (1976). Haitkin's subjective style is perfectly suited to the film's explosive climax where we're alongside Gallagher as he frantically pursues the alien through a hotel as security guards open fire on him.

Roger Ebert called *The Hidden* "a surprisingly effective film . . . a sleeper that talks like a thriller and walks like a thriller but has more brains than the average thriller." Hal Hinson of the *Washington Post* said the film was imbued with "punk soulfulness . . . a cop movie with an acute sense of B-movie play." Despite such laudatory reviews, the film turned only a small profit before disappearing from theaters. It's time for a reassessment. With *Invasion of the Body Snatchers*, Don Siegel proved that extraterrestrials and noir make for a potent and frightening brew. But *The Hidden* pushed the envelope even further with bizarre characters, supercharged set pieces, and genuinely unsettling ideas about humanity and identity. By the way, the next time some power-hungry politician perpetrates some perfidy . . . it might be wise to look to the skies. ∎

Keeper of the flame: MacLachlan literally opens fire on his intergalactic quarry as *The Hidden* speeds to its finale.

BOOK VS. FILM

M.T. Schwartzman

Film noir drew heavily on American pulp crime fiction for source material, but two notable films of the mid-twentieth century—*La Bête humaine* (1938) and *Human Desire* (1954)—trace their roots to a nineteenth-century novel by French naturalist writer Émile Zola. Both open aboard a locomotive speeding down the tracks—a steam model in the first, a sleek diesel in the second. Both remain true to the book in terms of plot, reordered a bit for dramatic effect and pared down to the main story line. However, with a change in time and place came changes in characters. These provide the key points of divergence between the two films, driven in large part by casting choices.

Written by Zola in 1889–90, *La Bête humaine* (literally translated as "the human beast") is a dark work whose content is violent, explicit, and bloody. At a time when Victorian authors in England like Anthony Trollope and William Makepeace Thackeray were writing polite novels of courtship, inheritance, and parliamentary politics, Zola was laying bare the soul of post-Napoleonic French society. His blunt realism, considered scandalous at the time, brought to light the deprivations and struggles of the working and lower classes—subjects often glossed over in popular novels meant for the general reading public. This unvarnished portrayal of the human condition became known as "naturalism" and is the author's most important literary contribution.

Zola's skill as a naturalist writer was especially evident in the vivid descriptions that filled his novels. His prose style, rich in linguistic brush strokes, has been compared to the paintings of the Impressionists, who were his contemporaries. His most famous body of work, the Rougon-Macquart series of sociopolitical novels, spanned twenty books covering alcoholism, prostitution, labor strife, and more. The author had a peculiar theory about heredity—specifically, that the tendency to kill could be passed down through generations. This theme is at the core of *La Bête humaine*, a noirish tale of adultery leading to murder. While most definitely nineteenth century in setting, style, and sociology, the story is of particular interest to devotees of film noir for its decidedly twentieth-century femme fatale.

When the story begins, we are introduced to Le Havre assistant stationmaster Roubaud and his doting wife, Séverine, who are occupying an apartment overlooking the Paris train depot during a short visit to the French capital. Roubaud has been called in on some railway business. While he conducts his affairs, he encourages Séverine to visit Grandmorin, her godfather and a director of the railway. Grandmorin has been something of a benefactor to the couple; he was partly responsible for Roubaud getting his position with the railway, and when he dies the couple will inherit his country house where Séverine spent part of her childhood.

Jean Gabin, here with Simone Simon, was the biggest star of the French poetic realist movement in the 1930s, known for his melancholy resignation and outbursts of explosive rage.

The third person in this emerging love triangle is train engineer Jacques Lantier, who harbors a dark secret: the sight of bare female flesh arouses in him neither passion nor lust, but murderous rage. Lantier enters the lives of Roubaud and Séverine after an amorous encounter with his cousin Flore goes horribly wrong, leaving him dazed and wandering the countryside. As luck (or fate) would have it, he crosses paths with an express train bound for Le Havre just as Roubaud and Séverine—passengers on the train—commit a brutal murder. This brings Lantier into the couple's web of deceit and sets him on a path to his own demise.

As the story progresses, we learn about Séverine's troubled past. Her godfather had sexually abused her, starting at age sixteen, and this awful fact sets the stage for a series of events that culminate not only in Grandmorin's death but also the revelation of a darker side of Séverine's nature as she plans another murder—that of her husband. "He was in the way, so you got rid of him," she reasons, "what could be more natural?" Victim has become predator.

The final characters in this tangled web are the trains. On a purely documentary level, Zola chronicled in detail and with great accuracy the workings of the national rail system as it crisscrossed the country, transforming French society—much as railroads did in Britain and the United States. On a symbolic level the trains and their tunnels are, of course, rife with erotic suggestiveness, as in this passage that puts Zola's painterly writing style on full display: "[Lantier] had been racing up and down the slopes for a long while when in front of him he saw the round opening of the tunnel, its black gaping mouth. An up-line train was disappearing into its depths, howling and whistling, and as it vanished, as though quaffed by the earth, it left behind one long shudder with which the ground continued to shake."

The French production of *La Bête humaine* was directed by Jean Renoir, who also wrote the script and plays a supporting role in the film as the accused laborer Cabuche. Having read the book in advance greatly enhances one's understanding of the movie, which communicates at least as

much through imagery and atmosphere as through language. This is especially true of the motivations behind the action, which are frequently driven by subconscious desires and impulses—according to Zola's sociological theories—and are not fully explained by the dialogue.

Lantier is portrayed by the understated Jean Gabin, whose roles often included proletarian antiheroes and who initiated the film, partly drawn to the project by his love of trains. Gabin's Lantier parallels Zola's—the misogynistic, homicidal rage is within him. He conveys also the "touchy and unsociable" demeanor that characterizes Lantier of the novel, only becoming animated—and even poetic—when talking about his beloved locomotive, Lison (La Lison in the book).

Séverine is brought to the screen by the coquettish Simone Simon. Lithe with a mane of thick, dark hair, she resembles the character as described by Zola and is equally manipulative, if not more so. When we first see her, she is framed by a window and gently stroking a white kitten—a clear allusion to her character's feline cunning.

Gloria Grahame and Glenn Ford in *Human Desire*, lensed by cinematographer Burnett Guffey who emphasized the characters' drab, bleak lives.

From that moment on, Simon's charismatic presence carries the picture.

Roubaud is played by Fernand Ledoux, a Belgian-born actor of French stage and screen who steps easily into the role of the railway functionary—affable enough when we first meet him, but quickly becoming sullen as he withdraws into a life of gambling. While the performance is serviceable, Ledoux's impact on the film is rather limited compared to that of his costars.

When Hollywood got a hold of the property in the mid-1950s, the title was changed to *Human Desire*, and German émigré Fritz Lang was installed at the helm as director. (This was his second time directing a Hollywood version of a film by Jean Renoir, since *Scarlet Street* [1945] had been based on Renoir's *La Chienne* [1931]). The screenwriter was Alfred Hayes (*Clash by Night* [1952]); the studio was Columbia Pictures. Fresh off *The Big Heat* (1953), his previous picture for Columbia made just the year before, Lang reunited the leads of that cast—Glenn Ford and Gloria Grahame—in his latest production. With them came a chemistry that supercharges the proceedings.

In conceiving this version of *La Bête*

humaine, producer Jerry Wald, Hayes, and Lang scrubbed clean the foreign elements of the book to create a distinctly American drama. They not only changed the title, but moved the setting to the East Coast, updated the period to soon after the Korean War, and—most importantly—made significant changes to his principal character. In the process, he crafted not a remake of the previous film but a new adaptation of the source novel.

Séverine, renamed Vicki Buckley, is played to perfection by Grahame in a nuanced performance that goes from fearful and vulnerable to cold-blooded. Roubaud's character (now Carl Buckley) reaches its full realization in the capable hands of veteran character actor and film noir stalwart Broderick Crawford, whose imposing physical presence brings an added dimension to the film's unabashed brutality and Hays Code–friendly ending.

Ford takes over the role of Lantier, renamed Jeff Warren. As the film opens, he is a veteran returning from three-plus years in Korea, and the "hereditary thirst for murder" is absent from his psyche. He is, at least when we meet him, the handsome and wholesome boy next door. The quintessen-

tial noir victim, he is soon drawn into a double life of secrecy and shadowy trysts. Jeff has a moral compass, though. When Vicki demands that he murder Carl, he balks:

"You've killed before," she challenges him, referring to his experiences in the war.

"Before?" he replies, "Oh, the war. I'd almost forgot. You thought I could do it because of that, huh? Well, there's a difference. In the war you fire into the darkness, something moving on a ridge—a position, a uniform, an enemy. But a man coming home helpless, drunk; that takes a different kind of killing."

"And a different kind of man," she responds.

And therein lies the critical difference: Lantier murders, Warren doesn't.

This was presumably a commercial choice. Audiences were unlikely to accept Glenn Ford as an adulterous murderer. But the influence of Zola's naturalism and determinism can still be felt; in Zola's view, people were products of their environment, their fates guided by circumstance. In this he foreshadowed the fatalism and entrapment of film noir, perfectly expressed by the vision of locomotives running on steel rails, to the end of the line. ∎

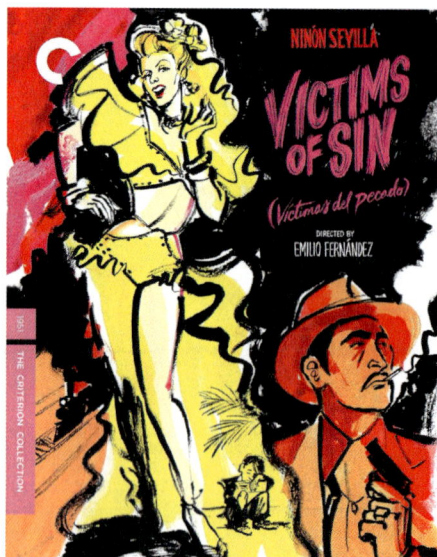

Victims of Sin (Criterion, Blu-ray, DVD)

My vote for the film noir (re)discovery of 2024 is this 1951 *cabaretera*, a genre of Mexican melodrama whose protagonists—sexy but good-hearted nightclub performers—battle predatory pimps, corrupt club owners, and poverty between energetic musical numbers. The incandescent Ninón Sevilla drives the film as Violeta, the star dancer of Club Changoo, a seedy but lively oasis of music, dance, and sex workers where the real-life mambo legend Pérez Prado conducts the house band. **Victims of Sin** packs plenty into 82 minutes: a vicious, preening pimp (Rodolfo Acosta); a dive into the sad, dusty alley of streetwalkers; a chivalrous hero (Tito Junco) who walks the streets trailed by his own mariachi band; plus motherhood, murder, vengeance, punishment, and redemption.

Filmmaker Emilio Fernández and cinematographer Gabriel Figueroa create a suitably noir palette for this world on the outskirts of the city, from the crowded, claustrophobic clubs to the railyards spewing pollution. But they also find a dignity in the sisterhood of performers and the working-class patrons of Violeta's second cabaret home. What could have been a tawdry tale of exploitation becomes a lively, resonant drama with an Afro-Cuban beat and a heroine whose compassion and decency never falter, even in the depths of her troubles.

The film was restored in 4K from a damaged 35mm camera negative in a collaboration between Mexico's Permanencia Voluntaria and Cinema Preservation Alliance in the United States. It showcases Figueroa's images and the Mexican and Afro-Cuban musical numbers beautifully.

EXTRAS: A vintage episode of the Mexican TV series *Those Who Made Our Cinema* tracing the history and legacy of *cabareteras* with film clips and an interview with Sevilla, plus new interviews with archivist Viviana García-Besné and cinematographer Rodrigo Prieto and an insert with an illuminating essay by Jacqueline Avila.

—*Sean Axmaker*

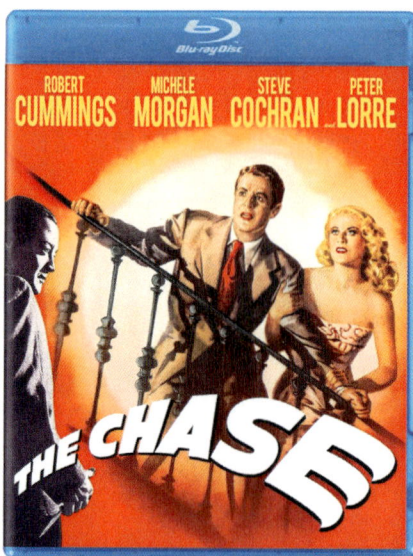

The Chase (Kino, Blu-ray)

Film noir is no stranger to unexpected twists and paranoid ordeals, but **The Chase** (1946) is in a class all its own. It starts with the casting of lightweight romantic lead Robert Cummings as Chuck Scott, a war vet on hard times working for a brutal gangster (Steve Cochran) and chauffeuring around the gangster's tormented wife (Michèle Morgan). She wants to escape and Scott obliges, until a Havana stopover spirals into a nightmarish conspiracy, with images to match by Franz Planer. Adapted from a Cornell Woolrich novel by Philip Yordan, the film was independently produced by Seymour Nebenzal, who ordered reshoots and restructured the narrative architecture. It all adds to the film's surreal, dreamlike quality; *The Chase* is one of the most delirious noirs ever made. It was restored in 2012 by the Film Foundation and first released by Kino in a superb edition in 2016. It's been newly remastered for this release and features a slightly upgraded image; the blacks are a touch deeper and the image has slightly increased clarity.

EXTRAS: Archival commentary by filmmaker Guy Maddin and two vintage radio adaptations of the Woolrich novel, carried over from the 2016 Blu-ray.

—*Sean Axmaker*

Pursued (Kino, Blu-ray)

Robert Mitchum plays an orphan haunted by jagged memories of a buried childhood trauma and hunted by a hateful one-armed man (Dean Jagger) in the most noir Western of the classic era. Mitchum is laconic and cool as the devoted adopted son of a protective widow (Judith Anderson), but behind his sleepy eyes is a tortured helplessness as everyone around him, including his adoptive family—steely Ma, resentful "brother" played by John Rodney (very Cain and Abel), and "sister"

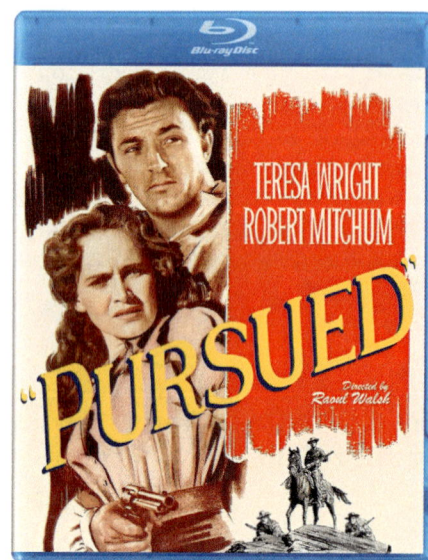

Teresa Wright (who loves him as more than a brother)—turn against him for reasons he can't comprehend until he finally confronts those primal memories. Directed by Raoul Walsh, it's a psychological thriller that plays like English Gothic fiction (with a helping of Biblical dimension) on the American frontier, roiling with hate, passion, jealousy, and obsessive vengeance. Cinematographer James Wong Howe's evocative imagery brings expressionist dimensions to the Western setting and pulls it into the shadows when the savage emotions explode in violence. Newly remastered from 4K scans of the original camera negative and other elements, the clarity shows in a superb image. A major upgrade from the earlier Olive Blu-ray.

EXTRAS: Commentary by NOIR CITY editor Imogen Sara Smith and an archival introduction by Martin Scorsese.

—*Sean Axmaker*

Film Noir: The Dark Side of Cinema XVII

[*Vice Squad* / *Black Tuesday* / *Nightmare*] (Kino, Blu-ray)

Edward G. Robinson headlines three independently produced crime dramas in this volume of Kino's long-running series. **Vice Squad** (1953) is a classic police procedural with Robinson driving the search for a cop killer, even if it means trampling the civil rights of an uncooperative witness. Director Arnold Laven goes through the

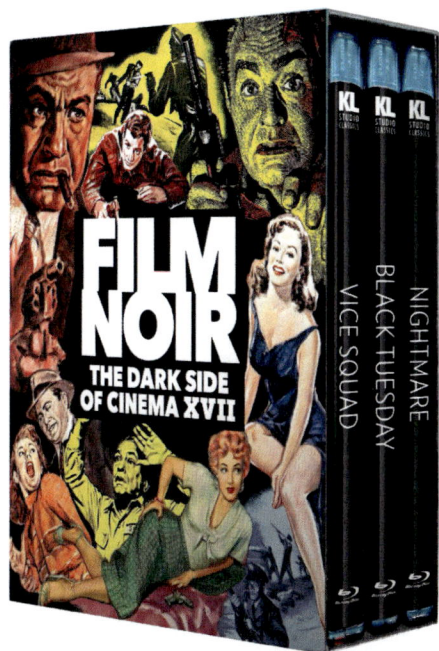

motions with more efficiency than distinction, but Robinson's understated authority is effective and Paulette Goddard injects snappy energy into her brief scenes as a savvy, flirtatious informant.

Maxwell Shane remakes of his own 1946 film *Fear in the Night* as **Nightmare** (1956), featuring Robinson as a police detective who thinks his musician brother-in-law (Kevin McCarthy) is imagining things until he stumbles upon a murder right out of his fevered dreams. It's based on a Cornell Woolrich novel and Shane leans into the paranoia and madness with the help of DP Joseph Biroc, who delivers spare yet striking expressionist images. The New Orleans setting is intriguing if underutilized—the few location shots make the generic studio sets look cheap—and bandleader Billy May appears as himself.

The set's standout is **Black Tuesday** (1954), a prison break thriller from director Hugo Fregonese and screenwriter Sydney Boehm that unleashes Robinson as a snarling gangster who masterminds an escape while on death row. Utterly mercenary and heartless aside from his love for Hatti, his girl on the outside (Jean Parker), Robinson's Vincent Canelli is ready to sacrifice anyone and everyone to get his hands on a fortune hidden by a fellow inmate (Peter Graves, practically reprising his role in *Night of the Hunter* [1955]). Fregonese cranks up the tension as the prisoners hole up with their hostages and shoot it out with the cops. Think of it as Robinson's *White Heat* (1949), playing a mercenary crime boss with an outsized presence and his own "top of the world" exit.

All three make their Blu-ray debuts in excellent new HD masters from archival elements.

EXTRAS: Commentary by Gary Gerani on **Vice Squad** and **Black Tuesday** and Jason Ney on **Nightmare**.

—*Sean Axmaker*

Upgrades

TO LIVE AND DIE IN L.A. (Kino, 4K UHD+Blu-ray) Kino gives William Friedkin's landmark neon noir, previously released in a terrific special edition Blu-ray from Shout! Factory, its 4K UHD debut. Mastered in 4K from the original camera negative, the colors feel burned into Robby Müller's sun-seared images and glow in the inky night scenes. Just gorgeous. No new

supplements; director commentary, interviews, documentary, and deleted scenes are all carried over from the 2003 DVD release and 2016 Shout! Factory Blu-ray. Worth the upgrade? Yes, for 4K viewers.

SCARLET STREET (Kino, 4K UHD+Blu-ray), mastered from a 35mm nitrate composite fine grain (courtesy of Universal Pictures and UCLA), improves upon the 2012 Blu-ray with a noticeably cleaner and slightly sharper image on both formats, plus new commentary by NOIR CITY editor Imogen Sara Smith.

Worth the upgrade? Yes.

ODDS AGAINST TOMORROW (Kino, Blu-ray) appears sourced from the same master as the earlier Olive release, but adds commentary by Alan K. Rode and archival Q&As with Harry Belafonte and Kim Hamilton.

Worth the upgrade? Yes.

HE WALKED BY NIGHT (Kino, Blu-ray) features a new HD master from a 16-bit 4K scan of the 35mm fine grain print, offering a slightly brighter image than the excellent 2017 Classic Flix release, and includes new commentary by NOIR CITY editor Imogen Sara Smith along with previously recorded commentary by Alan K. Rode and Julie Kirgo. The Classic Flix release, however, features an informative featurette and a booklet not in the Kino edition.

Worth the upgrade? Coin toss. ∎

—*Sean Axmaker*

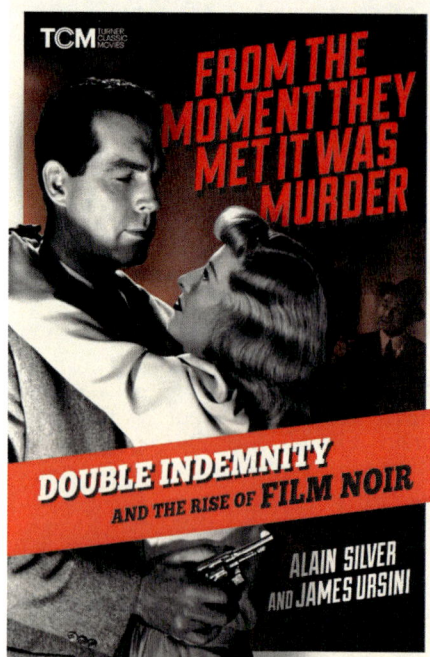

From the Moment They Met It Was Murder: *Double Indemnity* and the Rise of Film Noir

By Alain Silver and James Ursini
Running Press, April 2024
340 pages

Alain Silver and James Ursini are name brands in film noir. Over thirty years ago, their encyclopedia of the genre provided a template upon which much contemporary noir criticism has since been built. And in the ensuing decades, the duo has established a cottage industry of noir-related titles, publishing more than two dozen books related to the movement and classic Hollywood. *From the Moment They Met It Was Murder* is their newest offering, a well-illustrated trade hardcover. The book is a kitchen-sink omnibus of everything related to *Double Indemnity*, from the real-life crime that inspired James M. Cain's original novella to a roundup of the seventy years' worth of ink spilled on the film since its release in 1944.

Silver and Ursini take a fairly staid approach, succinctly summarizing various aspects of their subject. We get a section on the 1925 murder committed by Ruth Snyder and her lover, Henry Judd Gray, of Ruth's husband, Albert, which resulted in Snyder being one of the few women ever executed by the state of New York. Then we have mini biographies of the principal creative talents behind the film (source novelist Cain, writer-director Billy Wilder, and co-screenwriter Raymond Chandler), a recap of the casting and shooting, and an analysis of the analyses the film received upon its release and in the decades following. A jam-packed summary of the evolution of the classic noir movement serves as the book's coda—seemingly intended either to provide *Double Indemnity* with exhaustive context or top off a thin manuscript with greatest-hits material.

If this sounds like a somewhat dry summary of the book's contents, it's because the text itself is somewhat parched for passion. While it would be strange for someone wholly unfamiliar with *Double Indemnity* (novella or film) to sit down and read a book devoted to its history, the authors presume readers' excitement for the story without supplying an abundance themselves. While their forensic approach makes it difficult to zip through, the book does establish itself as an authoritative source for future researchers, complete with a cost analysis of the film's success, various accounts of Chandler's writing fee, the stage locations Paramount used for the Dietrichson home's interiors (Stages 8 and 9, in case you're wondering), and a line-by-line comparison of the script versus the recorded dialogue for Walter and Phyllis's meet-cute.

What comes through loud and clear amid the clutter of shooting dates and wardrobe details is that Wilder and Chandler's collaboration was a major enhancement of Cain's original story, resulting in an important and enduringly bleak film that mined the best qualities of everyone involved and helped kickstart the film noir cycle. Chandler's initial problem in adapting the novella was twofold: Cain's dialogue was overwritten and stagy and couldn't be used verbatim for the script, and Chandler wasn't the biggest fan of Cain's writing in the first place. One notable remark: "He is every kind of writer I detest . . . a Proust in greasy overalls."

Adding to Chandler's irritation was Wilder himself—an imp full of joie de vivre whose boisterous working style directly conflicted with Chandler's vibe as a pipe-clenching buzzkill. Thankfully, they recognized each other's talent even as they fought throughout their time working on the script, with Wilder acknowledging Chandler's vital role in the film's enduring legacy and the two happily never collaborating again.

The story of the casting provides many insights, including the fact that Wilder had to work to convince Stanwyck to do the film, as up to this point she had never played a role so diabolical. Dick Powell lobbied hard for the role of scheming insurance salesman Walter Neff—even agreeing to work for free in his pre–*Murder, My Sweet* yen to escape his hamster wheel of musicals—but Wilder wasn't convinced. And while Edward G. Robinson balked at his third-billed status, his reservations gave way when he learned that he'd be the highest paid of all the actors.

The analysis section is both the most infuriating and illuminating. Here the authors are in their element, dissecting generations of commentary, much of which was influenced by their own texts. We hear from such early writers in the field as Raymond Durgnat, Paul Schrader, Lowell Peterson, Janey Place, and Bob Porfirio, as well as feminist perspectives offered by Julie Grossman, Vivian Sobchack, Linda Brookover, and Elizabeth Ward. While the flow of these opinions sometimes feels all over the place, it's nice to get a CliffsNotes-style rundown of viewpoints, ranging from "Walter Neff is seduced not just by a woman, Phyllis Dietrichson the 'femme fatale,' but also by the homosocial fantasy that he can compete with Keyes" (Grossman) to Imogen Sara Smith's canny observation that "Phyllis has murdered to get her dream home, and now is ready again to murder to escape it. The dark, somber furnishings . . . and the dim, dusty lighting in these interiors create the sense of a suffocating tomb."

The coda summary of the classic noir movement is dizzying in its references, and serves as an excellent infomercial for Silver and Ursini's still-authoritative *Film Noir:*

The Encyclopedia, a must-own for any devotee. And while *From the Moment They Met It Was Murder* may be more suited to the home library than the nightstand, it's a welcome reminder the while the hunt for the rarest of the rare is all well and good, it's just as important to go back to the basics, reacquainting ourselves with the films that got us hooked on these dark streets in the first place.

—*Rachel Walther*

Edges of Noir: Extreme Filmmaking in the 1960s

By Michael Mirabile
Berghahn Books, February 2024
280 pages

Though it has been the subject of much discussion, the end point of classic noir remains a fascinating topic. *Touch of Evil* (1958) has long stood as the benchmark, an uber-noir that seemingly leaves no territory to explore. But *Odds Against Tomorrow*, released the following year, did just that as a groundbreaking heist film that addresses racism and the African American experience while incorporating a noir style that is both innovative and classical. That said, whether noir did in fact end in the late 1950s is debatable, with artists outside the Hollywood studio system contributing raw entries that bookend the coming decade: Allen Baron's *Blast of Silence* (1961) and Leonard Kastle's *The Honeymoon Killers* (1970). Both offer tones in keeping with traditional noir even if they stray from motifs of the 1940s and 1950s.

With several studies of both 1950s film noir and the neo-noir cycle (1973–81) available, the transitional period of the 1960s calls for further exploration. In *Edges of Noir*, Michael Mirabile argues that this decade is the era of late noir, with compelling readings of fourteen films as social commentary (though unfortunately, he does not include the Baron or Kastle films cited above). Mirabile first looks at 1950s noirs that invoke paranoia with atomic age themes. Their sense of irresolution, he argues, and occasional borrowing from other genres led to transitional noir films in the 1960s. The author begins by reading *D.O.A.* (1949) as a victim-turned-avenger noir that resolves the crime against Frank Bigelow (Edmond O'Brien) but little of the growing societal panic associated with it. It

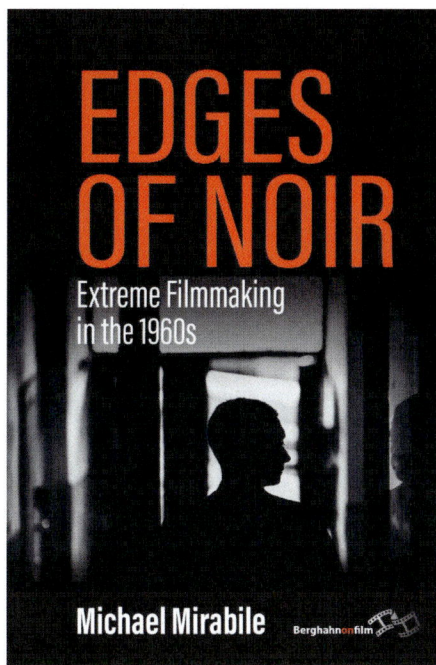

is a pivotal film that looks back at the early noir films of the 1940s while its cumulative terror, despite its plot resolution, foreshadows treatments in coming years. Moving on to *Invasion of the Body Snatchers* (1956), *My Son John* (1952), and *Psycho* (1960) (chapter two), Mirabile risks disapproval from noir purists yet clarifies strains in the films' exposure of the dark side of everyday complacency.

The book offers standout discussions of writer-director Samuel Fuller in the following chapters. *Underworld U.S.A.* (1961) serves as a bridge into more challenging territory for Fuller, while Mirabile reads *Shock Corridor* (1963) (in chapter three) as the high point in a series of "clinical-carceral" films featuring protagonists who enter a psychiatric hospital under false pretenses for a scheme involving performance (in *Shock Corridor*, to solve a murder). Fuller's journalist-investigator soon finds himself trapped, in a timely style echoing Korean War veterans returning home for physical and psychological treatment. Chapter four analyzes the tabloid/exploitation traditions in *The Naked Kiss* (1964) while connecting it to the 1950s exposés of the dark underbelly, as a noir that "[effaces] some of the obsessively inscribed lines . . . such as that between 'normal' and 'deviant' behavior."

Characteristically well researched, chapter five offers a welcome surprise with a discussion of noir innovator Edward Dmytryk's *Mirage* (1965), which "[reflects] on the vexed place of film noir amid the altered cultural and media landscapes of the

1960s." The film's postmodern treatment—one invoking various styles of the thriller—depicts a bleak media-saturated milieu, effectively halted by a skyscraper blackout that launches a tortuous plot. Its noir allusions notwithstanding, Mirabile accounts for the film's chaos as signaling fears of catastrophe, i.e., the A-bomb. Chapter six details the changing femme fatale/vamp in the 1960s through the author's rephrasing of Freud's female binary, i.e., the heteronormative male's tendency to compartmentalize women in either "Madonna" or "mistress" categories (though Freud is carefully not referred to throughout the book). In an especially loose interpretation of noir, Mirabile argues that *A Rage to Live* (1965) refracts "the bizarre oneiric landscape of *Marnie*" through melodrama, while the sexual indiscretions of newspaper heiress Grace Caldwell (Suzanne Pleshette) result in her being a victim to a "conjugal captor." The discussion, paired with one on Alfred Hitchcock's film, seems better suited to an analysis of Cold War family melodrama than noir. A closing chapter on John Boorman's *Point Blank* (1967), as an experimental noir "spectacle" that eyes late-1960s counterculture, is enjoyable if less perceptive and surprising. This sign-off with a fan favorite will leave readers thinking of the film more as an early neo-noir, consciously injecting experimentation into an of-its-time tribute to victims-turned-avengers, as in *D.O.A.*

The conclusion suggests that stronger thrillers from the 1970s, like *The French Connection* (1971) and *The Friends of Eddie Coyle* (1973), bridge the gap between late noir and the decade's genre-conscious neo-noirs. Despite the quibbles touched on here, *Edges of Noir* makes a strong case for the 1960s as the late-age proper. At Mirabile's best, his focus is informed by elements outside of film noir, especially pulp paperbacks, with little sense of digression. The contextual passages will get heavy for some, but the focus on the films is rewarding for those willing to put in the effort. ∎

—*Matthew Sorrento*

NOIR CROSSWORD

Leading Man

Rich Taus

ACROSS

1. Create a part for an actor
5. 17. Across film about the CIA precursor (1946)
8. Bombards with email
13. "Guilty" or "not guilty"
14. 1950 noir with a luminous toxin
15. List of mistakes
17. Leading man with a boyish-sounding name
19. Thick-skinned relative of lemons
20. Actress Lathan or Yemen capital
21. "___ Stop," 1956 Monroe film
22. "The ___ Star," 1957 Western
23. Video game fig. not controlled by a human
25. Lake that appears in several 17. Across films
27. Like 14. Across in 1988
30. Site for a fight
31. Edible tuber of the Andes
32. Adjective for Sydney Greenstreet
34. Bacall's nickname in "To Have and Have Not" (1944)
38. With 40. Across, breakout film for 17. Across (1942)
40. See 38. Across
43. Napoleon of U.N.C.L.E.
44. Part of MGM
46. "Serial ___," 1994 black comedy
47. Round before the finals
50. De Niro's role in "The Untouchables" (1987)
52. "My ___ Brunette," 1947 noir parody with a 17. Across cameo
55. Part of Dickie Moore's prep for "Out of the Past" (1947)
56. 1927-1960, Hollywood's Golden ___
57. "Knock on ___ Door," Bogart noir (1949)
58. What you do with buds
62. Title role for Lanza in a 1951 biopic
64. "The ___," 17. Across film (1942), Hammett book
67. "___ Tailor Soldier Spy" (2011)
68. Rhyming synonym of flick
69. Workplace for Doc and Dopey
70. Requires
71. Workplace for 17. Across
72. Menace in "Them!" (1954)

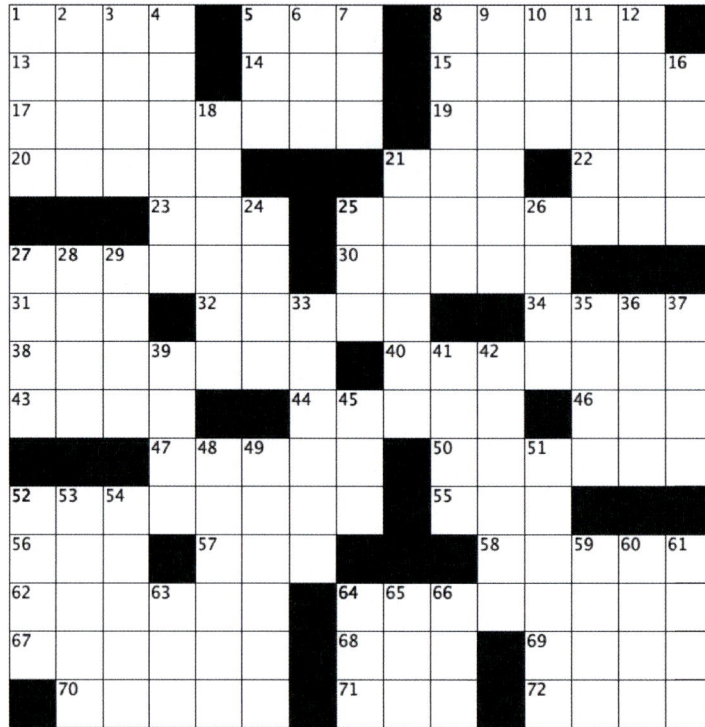

DOWN

1. Tax pros
2. Earthen stew pot
3. Scorsese's "___ Streets" (1973)
4. Fruit in the song "Day-O"
5. ___ Mae, Oscar-winning role for Whoopi
6. Turf
7. Blue
8. Safe
9. Stir
10. Carney of neo-noir "The Late Show" (1977)
11. Cuban hero with an eponymous airport
12. Adjective for a 17. Across role
16. Actress ___ May Wong
18. Maltese animal (no, not the bird)
21. Deprived
24. Philippine island, anagram of "cube"
25. ___ deferens
26. Humorous poet Ogden
27. Goes bad
28. Reverberate
29. Suffix for "black" in film noir
33. Bad blood
35. Red carpet ride
36. "___ Man," 2008 Robert Downey Jr. vehicle
37. Humorous video
39. Meh
41. Black and white killer
42. Comedy Central tributes
45. Opposite direction from WNW
48. Rubbed out
49. "Bull Durham" (1988) milieu
51. Matter that's not solid, liquid, or gas
52. ___-checking, a task writing these clues
53. "Dead ___," (1991) Branagh/Thompson neo-noir
54. Creator of Nemo and Fogg
59. Restricted sight under the Hays Code
60. Portable shelter
61. "___ of Laura Mars" (1978)
63. Luau strings
64. A Brit might call it satnav
65. Commit perjury
66. Appear in a film noir

© May 5, 2024

For solution, go to filmnoirfoundation.org

Made in the USA
Middletown, DE
19 September 2024